THE SUMMER CHILDREN

Bernadette M Redmond

DEDICATED TO MARTIN KEARNS

1901 – 1985

'In life you should play the hand you're given and not waste time wishing that you had something else'.

Other memoirs

I Dreamt I Dwelt in Marble Halls

Thrown on Life's Surge

Pea Soup and Jellied Eels

A Promise of Tomorrows

ACKNOWLEDGEMENTS

I would like to thank several members of the family and friends for taking me down memory lane and sharing their knowledge of family lore. Sarah Madden, Maureen Qualter, Bridgie Glynn nee Duggan, Eileen Cullinan and my brother Seán Redmond are now deceased, but Mary King nee Carr, Una Cullinan, Seoirse Morris and Sheila Forde nee Kelly are still with us, and long may they remain so.

Bean Sí (banshee or bean-sidhe) artist unknown

Table of Contents

Chapter 1 The Road from Dublin

Chapter 2 Seanmháthair Loftus

Chapter 3 The Cloonbiggen house

Chapter 4 Learning the business

Chapter 5 Lighten our darkness

Chapter 6 Evening in Paris

Chapter 7 Bedtime in Cloonbiggen

Chapter 8 Language Barriers

Chapter 9 The Staff of Life

Chapter 10 The Bog Road

Chapter 11 Gortcloonmore

Chapter 12 An Unusual Happening

Chapter 13 The Cregboy Cousins

Chapter 14 The Radar Station

Chapter 15 In the name of God

Chapter 16 Dear God in Heaven

Chapter 17 The Doctor Calls

Chapter 18 Lime Washing

Chapter 19 Wives and Daughters

Chapter 20 Family Reunion

Chapter 21 The Galway Races

Chapter 22 Journeys End

Chapter 22 Waking the Dead

Chapter 23 Post Mortem

Chapter 24 The Jaunting Car

Chapter 25 Slán agus Beannacht

Chapter 26 Uncovering Dublin

Chapter 27 Changing times

Chapter 28 Bina's

Chapter 29 God's Bounty

Chapter 30 Loughgeorge

Chapter 31 God Willing

Chapter 32 The Day the Canon Roared

Chapter 33 Unsettling Times

Chapter 34 Intimations of mortality

Chapter 35 The Eye of the Storm

Chapter 36 Thou Shalt Not

Chapter 37 Die on your Feet

Chapter 38 The Fainne

Chapter 39 Soldiers of Christ

Chapter 40 The Copper Vase

Chapter 41 The Enigma

Chapter 42 Requiescat in pace et Amor

Chapter 1; The Road from Dublin

The long car journey was nearly over. Our driver, Christy Clinton, who bore a passing resemblance to Humphrey Bogart, was as unperturbed and cheerful as when we had left Dublin seven hours earlier. The 126 Irish miles to Co. Galway, with stops to enable my father to indulge in liquid refreshment, and us children to explore the revolting 'toilet' facilities in bona fide hostelries, would not have taken the average car driver seven hours in 1944, but Uncle Christy, a year married to the Da's sister, Sheila, was no ordinary driver. He considered himself a good driver, a careful driver, a courteous driver, but to every other driver on the road he was a menace, implanting murderous impulses in their hearts and creating red mists of rage to cloud their powers of rational thought.

Uncle Christy was probably the originator of road rage. When he drove, he took up pole position in the middle of the road, progressing at a stately twenty five miles an hour in his shiny black 1938 Ford Fordor car, never overtaking or pulling over, ever mindful of wandering sheep and cattle, suicidal dogs, horse and carts, hay laden tractors, the lame and the halt, the mad, the bad and the sad and sundry other hazards that might require an emergency stop. Not that he ever had to make a emergency stop, due to his hyper vigilance we always has plenty of time to come to a rolling halt.

In concentrating on driving with due care and attention he happily ignored the orchestra of honking horns and the curses of fellow road users who cut in, or overtook him, and he seemed oblivious to the sins of blasphemy he was responsible for, from normally reasonable and easy going Irish drivers. What any of us were doing driving across Éire, as it was then called, where strict rationing was in force, was not a question that interested a young child.

As soon as the grandeur of the Claregalway Friary ruins came into view my heart began to race, and my stomach tie itself in knots of anticipation. When we came up to the turn for Cloonbiggen the sight of the De Burgo Keep on the far shore of the River Clare revealed itself. The sun broke forth after a passing shower throwing out the colours of golden lichen that clothed its grey time-beaten stones, contrasting with the dark green of the ivy that wandered up its walls and around its windows and corbelled parapet and the brilliant green of the umbelliferous plants that clustered around its feet. It vied in its feudal beauty in harmony of colour and form with the ecclesiastical ruins facing it.

The car turned right onto the bog road putting the Friary on our left and as it rocked and jolted along this rutted sun dried boreen, my eyes were on the flat horizon ahead, and the enormous blue sky with its occasional thin wispy cirrus cloud. We passed the Connell's farmhouse on the right and saw Maggie in the yard turning to look at the unusual sight of a car down in Cloonbiggen. Doctor, Priest, soldier, the select groups allowed a petrol ration, the query was in her stance as she put up her hand to shade her eyes, but the grapevine had been busy, and as she recognized us, she waved.

Further in the road we glimpsed the Holland house through fuchsia bushes, uncut hawthorns, blackthorns and bramble hedges, nearly missing the right hand turn that hid my grandmothers small thatched cottage from view until we pulled up outside. But I had smelt it before I caught a glimpse of the house, the turf fire.

When I would return to Dublin in eight weeks time my clothes and belongings would be impregnated with that musty earthy smell, and despite my mother's attempts to eradicate it with lavender bags, and eucalyptus leaves from the Botanical Gardens it would cling on in my Sunday best woolen coat well up to Christmas Mass.

As we slowed down, a black and white collie came from nowhere and tried to bite lumps out of Christy's tires. For a man who had calmly and serenely, driven across Éire, no culchie cur was going to destroy *his* tyres, so he leapt out of the car like a man possessed, forgetting as he did so to engage the handbrake.

Luckily our screams woke my befuddled father who managed to halt the car inches from a three foot ditch draining the meadow opposite the house.

The dog vanished.

Chapter 2; Seanmháthair Loftus

Granny Loftus, born Mary Bridget Qualter in Gortcloonmore in 1870, was my maternal grandmother. She was a widow since the spring of 1933 when her husband Tom Loftus had keeled over while setting potatoes. His death on a gusty day was said to have been caused by a 'poc-sidhe' or fairy stroke regardless of the fact that the death certificate documented apoplexy. At seventy three my grandmother was still a good looking woman, tall for Irish peasant stock, and had the Qualter good bone structure, humorous dark eyes, straight well shaped nose and pale skin. Her once dark hair, now grey was worn twisted into a bun and held with hairpins.

Known as 'Mavoureen' within the family she was a capable woman who kept a neat little farm, renting out a few acres of meadow land to make ends meet. She seldom ventured outside her little domain, not even to take the Saturday Market bus into Galway. She had two grown children under her roof, so like any farmers wife her working day was long.

She had obviously got tired waiting for us, since it was now well past five o'clock, and although the top half of the front door was open there was no sign of her. Bridie, my younger sister, and I got out of the car, calling to her, while my father and Christy emptied the vehicle of cases and parcels. The yard was full of vocal hens clucking to each other, and a large strutting cockerel who warned the neighbourhood of our presence. I loved the different sounds that hens made going about their business and when they were settling down for the night. We heard a distant cry of 'tiuc – tiuc - tiuc' and running around the side of the house saw Seanmháthair up the field looking for out layers eggs. Between us and her was a very irate gander and we just made it over the gate into the field as he swooped down on us to peck us to death. She smiled and nodded in satisfaction at our arrival but showed no overt signs of affection, hampered as she was by an upturned apron full of eggs held clutched with one hand and a long hazlewood staff for warding off the gander in the other. Steering the puffed up hissing gander into the field she welcomed the two men formally in Gaelic, they only being related to her by marriage, and said dryly to Christy 'Well at least you made it in time for the *six o'clock* Angelus' The humour in the remark was lost on him. She had obviously been expecting us around noon when the church bell would toll the mid day Angelus. She might not have heard the bell muted by a miles distance, because, like old Breton Law, distances were measured by the travelling of sound. An alarm raised by Bina's ass at the sound of the church bell would travel to the cawing crows in the Friary bell tower and on to the Connells, Holland's and Greally cockerels thereafter setting off the Feeney's dog.

Gauging the time she would stop whatever she was doing to bless her self and recite the Angelus. It was an era when people were not ruled by timepieces but by the hours available between dusk and dawn, the weather, and the cycle of the seasons, and if you prided your life down a dark bog road, enough money to buy carbide crystals to light your bicycle lamp.

She reached in and unbolted the bottom half of the front door and we followed her into the main room of the cottage. The gloom inside was initially in stark contrast to the bright sunny evening outside.

Chapter 3; The Cloonbiggen House

The thick stone walls had small recessed windows three at the front of
the house and two to the rear. Apart from that, unless the front, back or
bedroom doors were open there was no other natural light. There was no
ceiling to the room which gave it height. The roof rafters were exposed
and intertwined by hazel hurdles. This structure held the thatch in place.
As my eyes became accustomed to the gloom I noted with delight that
nothing had changed. The dresser still stood against the back wall with its
shining mismatched delph and jugs that my Dublin Granny would have
scorned. Next to it was an oblong scrubbed kitchen table, now covered
with a white lace trimmed table cloth, with a small bunch of hand
embroidered roses in each corner. Pushed tidily underneath each side of
the table were four kitchen chairs. Supplementary seating was provided
by three short stools with rush woven seats, none of which sat squarely
on the cement floor. They had originally been normal size but several
attempts at curing the rocking had taken inches off them. The big folded
up settle bed, painted a faded Dutch blue, was against the wall to the left,
and just beyond it the door to the 'big bedroom' that Uncle Séameen and
Martin Kearns shared. Hanging on the wall beyond it was the only object
in the room that interested me. A small wooden housheen barometer
with two doors that showed a girl in a pink dress with a parasol indicating
fine weather and a boy in blue with an umbrella forecasting rain. Neither
of them was brave enough to step out of their doorway to proclaim the
weather for the day. For that we had to depend on Uncle Martin,
Seanmháthair's brother.

The floor level hearth was the main feature of the room and was ideal
for burning turf. The turf sat on iron rods, under which was dug a
shallow pit for falling ashes. This pit was cleared out daily its contents
kept dry in a box in the barn to be added to soil to release potash to
enhance the potato crop. The glowing embers, known as gríosach, were
kept going even when the turf fire had been allowed to die down because
of the heat of the day. Placed to the side of the fire they were needed for
stewing a pot of tea, to cook the potato cakes on a floured griddle, or

heaped on the lid of the pot oven when baking bread. In time I learned the necessary dexterity in the use of long handled thongs to make a good circular gríosach,

The hearth had in-built stone seats with a thin feather filled, hessian covered, embroidered, cushion on each for meager comfort. Bolted onto the back wall was a long piece of cast iron with a hinged arm, which swung out like a crane over the fire, and heated the water in the half gallon cast iron kettle, or cooked the contents of an enormous three, legged, lidded, cooking pot. On either side of the hearth were two latched doors, one leading to my grandmother's bedroom, facing the back of the house, and one to my Aunt Sarah's room with a view out the front.

When the house was built a piece of old bog oak had been fashioned into a lintel cum over mantel in the stone wall above the hearth instead of the traditional arched lode stones. Placed at either end of the mantel were two paraffin lamps, waiting for dusk. It would be another twenty years before electricity came to Cloonbiggen. Beneath the front window was a small round table with a lace doily to protect the wood from any spillage from a jug full of marigolds and margaritas. Nailed on the wall by the front door was a porcelain holy water font, an Angel with outstretched wings tipped in gold, looking pensively down into the little font in front of him, and above the door was a St Brigit's cross, the rushes fading since it's renewal in February and a piece of cordalyne palm, still green, from Palm Sunday.

The back door opened into a small scullery leading to the real back door which was built not to be in line with the front door and opened outwards to the left. Hanging on right side wall was a large zinc bath and a washboard, and from ceiling hooks were two dead hares and a half leg of cured bacon. In the corner was a creel of turf to keep the fire going. On a small square table sat a butter churn, a covered pail of water and a sack of flour, and underneath it a large iron three legged cooking pot and its draining skib. On a shelf above was a selection of fire blackened pots and pans. The window in the back wall of the scullery faced the front door and looked out on a well kept vegetable plot and a field drilled with potatoes, and beet. However both its inside and outside sills were so full of geraniums that the view was nonexistent. Outside the back door was a crusheen and a chipped green iron mangle which saw service every Monday, washday. On the wall, protected by the overhang of the thatch was a small mesh doored press, painted the same faded Dutch blue as the settle. This press was both fridge and larder but usually held little more than milk, butter and eggs.

There was no clock in the house but an old pendulum clock sat broken in one of the cribs out in the barn. It had seen several coats of paint, probably one for each time the Stations had been said in the house.

Having satisfied myself that all was as I remembered my mind turned to food. Despite protestations from the men that they were not hungry the smell of frying bacon and eggs, accompanied by mushrooms picked in the dew of the morning, potato cakes and homemade soda bread soon had them sitting at the table with their knives and forks at the ready. Bridie and I had hen fresh boiled eggs and potato cakes slathered with butter. Tea was a commodity not squandered on children so glasses of buttermilk were placed in front of us.

My father and Christy were spending the night at Aunt May's house, one of my mother's sisters, and Seanmháthair's thirty three year old middle daughter. Married to Mick Duggan, they lived in Cregboy, out on the road to Galway a couple of miles away. Both of them were anxious to be on their way, and young as I was I had known Granny Loftus was not taken in by their eagerness to get there. She had told them that Séameen, and Sarah, her unmarried son and daughter were out making hay with the Concannon's. With the fine weather the process from cutting the hay to making hay would be short because, with the grace of God and his Holy Mother, the hay would not need to be turned. In a wet year the whole process could take up to two weeks and anybody big enough to wield a pike was pressed into service for this labour intensive task. We also learned from Seanmháthair that if the weather remained good the corn cutting could be started as early as the week after the Galway Races.

During the Emergency, as World War II was known, there were official regulations in place regarding the percentage of arable land that had to be tilled, and each farmer had to fulfill his quota of growing wheat, oats and barley for the Department of Agriculture. This edict was met with much resentment, and a certain amount of hardship, since it was done at the expense of good husbandry. In an era before sprays, farmers who knew their land would leave it fallow every few years to let the land recover, but they were currently not allowed to do so. Although they were guaranteed a Government price, it did not meet the price they would normally get, nor did they reach the yield they would expect from rested land.

The Da and Christy being Dubliners were not au fait with country expectations so would have been deemed ill mannered by Seanmháthair. They made no effort to observe the rituals and traditions of local hospitality which was to exhaust every subject under the sun until one got to the heart of the matter by circumlocution, to garner the news you wanted to hear. Giving them up as a bad job she saw them on their way telling them that everybody would work on while there was light, before the men adjourned to Bina Lenihan's Pub. This gave them a choice of heading straight to Bina's or driving on to Aunt May's and running the risk spending an evening of circumlocution with *her*.

They choose the former, but seeing no sign of Uncle Mick they headed onwards for Cregboy on strict instructions from Bina, a niece of Seanmháthair's, for all three of them to come back. This they did having paid their respects to Aunt May and getting caught in Mary Casserly's web, the latter treating them as fair game for an hour's entertainment but more of which anon. Sabina Lenihan's grandfather, Thomas, and Seanmháthair's mother, Bridget, were brother and sister. Bina's branch became Lenihans while our branch remained Lenehans so for those of you reading this, it's not *my* spelling that's at fault.

Chapter 4; Learning the Business

As soon as the men had gone Granny Loftus took Bridie and I across the cobbled yard to the left of the house, past the water tank and trough, the mossy white washed barn and pig shed, and around the back of the hen and duck houses, and out of sight of the road , to 'do our business'. In a world without water closets, or even makeshift latrines our excretory products were not wasted. Urinating was easy, chose a corner by the soiled straw waiting to go on the manure heap, and cover the product of your kidneys with a handful of dry straw. Defecating was more problematic because you had to choose a place where nobody was going to walk, somewhere the pigs wouldn't rootle it up, where the territorial gander did not consider it to be within his defensible boundaries, and where there was a good supply of dock leaves necessary for wiping your bum and applying to places lacerated by nettles. In bad weather the right hand back corner of the barn could be used. At night, if nature called, the chamber pot under the bed was pressed into service. I have no recollection of ever washing my hands afterwards, a factor no doubt, in conjunction with drinking untreated water and visits to Bina's kitchen that resulted in a hardiness that set me up for life.

For children bathing and hair washing took place on Friday evening in the scullery and involved a tin bath, gallons of hot water and a rota defined by age, the same water being used by all.

Although I refer to her as Granny Loftus we addressed her as *Seanmháthair*, meaning Grandmother in Irish, but talked about her as Granny Loftus to differentiate her from Granny Redmond, known as 'The Gran' my father's mother, Julia Byrne, in Dublin. The definite article was an indication of *her* importance in our lives. After doing our business we helped Seanmháthair gather in the ducks for the night and a few straggling hens. The gander she left for Aunt Sarah to round up later. We fed the sow and three well grown noisy bonhams a mixture of boiled potatoes, cabbage leaves and beet pulp which they gobbled up noisily and greedily squinting up at us seeking more.

Chapter 5; Lighten our darkness

It was still light so Bridie and I set out to explore our surroundings. We were given no dire warnings except not to wander into the bog, to close any gates we opened, and to be home before dark. At five and a half, and three and a quarter we were city wise kids who could hold our own, and were perceptive enough to know that straying from the boreen could get us lost or sucked down into the bog. Getting back before dark was assured, because if we were not, the *Bean Sí* would get us. We also knew never to pick up a comb from the ground because she would have left it to tempt us before she spirited us away.

We walked as far as the dead oak tree known as the *Bean Sí's* tree at the T junction with the road back to Claregalway to the left, and the road ahead leading into the bog and the red and orange sky over Gortcloonmore, where a small nest of families lived. One of the families, the Qualter's were my mother's cousins, our grandmother Mary Bridget Qualter and Martin Qualter, were sister and brother, two of a large family of children born to my great grandparents, Bridget Lenehan of Gortadooey and Thomas Qualter of Gortcloonmore.

Martin, and his wife, known as' Bid Noone from Cloon' lived in the old Qualter family house, built in my great grandparents time. They had five unmarried, grown up children Tom, Malachy, Maureen, Winnie and Johnny. Johnny was already twenty and not very interested in entertaining children but Malachy, known as Lackie, and Winnie, were great fun, and we hoped that harvesting would not make it too late for them to cycle over to see us before we went to bed. Maureen worked in Galway and only came home on her day off, and Tom worked for the County Council, so we saw little of them.

Just as we were turning for home we saw a cyclist in the distance weaving along like as drunken sailor. On closer inspection we identified the 'drunk' as Winnie Qualter, concentrating on circumnavigating the ruts, and despite being a calm evening, looking out for little whirls of dust cloud moving along the road. This could be a band of *sidhe-gaoithe* or wind fairies travelling from one *Lis* to another. It was best to step out of their way because though generally benign the *Sidhe* could put a curse on you if you annoyed them, and they regarded interfering with their journey with serious displeasure.

Winnie was an athletic pretty girl of twenty two and was a mighty catch for somebody who wouldn't worry about the lack of a dowry. When we got the hugs and the Céad Míle Fáilte romhat abhaile's out of the way I noticed the rush basket at the front of the bike had a small churn of milk well lashed to the handle bar. Winnie, we discovered, was on a mission of mercy with the milk and the contents of a shoebox box strapped on the rear carrier rack. Bicycles in those days were big, heavy and at least twenty years old, with a single gear, and a chain guard if you were lucky. There were no refinements such as panniers for transporting goods, so it was not an unusual sight to see the rider festooned with brown paper parcels, or a woman riding a man's bike for the added convenience of carrying a child, or goods, on the cross bar. Taking care of your inner tubes meant the difference between walking and riding because during the Emergency they were impossible to replace, and repair kits were like gold dust.

It was from Winnie that we learned that Seanmháthair's cow had died. The death of Granny Loftus's Kerry Black a week before was not only a financial blow, but had daily practical repercussions milk being necessary for making butter, producing buttermilk, making bread, rearing calves and feeding the skimmed milk to the pigs. A new cow meant money had to be found, and in a community based on mutual help, self sufficiency and a system of bartering not much money changed hands, nor was there a great need for money, so finding a means of earning some was not easy.

When we reached the house there was a bicycle outside. Nobody had passed us on the road so whoever it was has come in from Loughgeorge or used the short cut across Connell's land. 'Tis the divil himself' said Winnie as her brother Lackie appeared in the doorway. Bridie and I were giddy with excitement at the sight of him. At twenty seven he had the thin muscular frame of a hard working agricultural worker used to physical work. His Qualter good looks and resemblance to Winnie and Seanmháthair stamped him as family. Bridie and I had missed out on this gene pool and were Redmond's to the core, shorter limbs, bigger heads, blue eyes and brown hair. While their pale skin took on a natural tan during whatever fine weather there was, our melanin deficient skin freckled and burned to a crisp at a hint of sun. Depending on the season of the year we went from blue, to white, to pink, speckled, to red, and then peeled.

Lackie had come in the back of Connell's farm. Although he had been hay making since dawn up in Cregboy with Pat Cullinan and Mick Duggan, he was as cheerful and funny as ever, bringing news and gossip from every townland in Claregalway. At a time when families could not afford a wet and dry battery radio, and only read the weekly *Connacht Tribune* second or third hand, and well past it's sell by date, a visit from Lackie was better than any seven o'clock news from Radio Éireann. His genuine interest in people, lively mind and lack of maliciousness meant that people told him things they might have had no intention of disclosing, even in the confessional, (particularly in Canon Moran's time), if so, you're secret was safe with Lackie. But the news of pregnancies, births, marriages, deaths, match making, the price of land, the yield of hay, the availability of paraffin, and most importantly, the price livestock was fetching and who would be selling, were Lackies stock in trade. He was a good solid worker and a great raconteur. His anecdotes were legendry but often went over my head. It was years before I got the one about a girl falling off her bicycle and the wedding bouquet covering her bump or the equally obscure 'he's gone out to turn his bicycle' if somebody discreetly disappeared up the haggard. Those who knew him still talk about him with the greatest affection. He carried the milk churn into the scullery and Winnie took a bowl of butter wrapped in muslin out of the shoe box. Thanks and blessings were showered on her, and the same to be taken back to her mother, Bid.

 Seanmháthair swung the long hinged iron arm holding the hooked-on big blackened kettle over the fire to bring it to the boil while Winnie set the table for supper   She then reached forward to feed the glowing fire but Winnie told her to 'Suigh síos agus lig do scíthe' and set about removing some small embers, placing them to the side while she banked fresh sods of turf in a wigwam shape on top of the remaining embers, using the long handled thongs with a surety that denoted long practice.

She tipped up the boiling kettle flushing the fire scorched teapot before putting a measure of tea leaves into the scalded pot, putting it on a small trivet to draw.

We heard the gander's protest before we heard voices through the open half door and then footsteps coming up the front path. Peter and his sister Bin-e Greally, kin to Bid Greally still in Gortcloonmore, had come along the road to be the first neighbours to welcome us. They settled in with a 'Bail ó Dhia anseo' to the adults, and a 'Tá tú fáilte roimh' and a handshake to Bridie and me before Bin-e's inquisition about life at home began.

Dusk was now falling but no lamp had yet been lit. Our faces, formerly brightened by the glowing embers were now, like the rest of us put into shadow by the newly banked turf. Winnie took down the paraffin lamp, removing the globe to adjust the wick, and with a quill of paper lit from the fire; put the flame to the wick and the lamp was lit. While Winnie placed the lamp on the table I noticed that Lackie had not come with one arm as long as the other. Two candles had been unwrapped from a half page of a month old news paper which had been folded and put to one side for perusal in daylight. Candles might seem an odd offering to bring, but paraffin was rationed and of poor quality.

Although Éire was a neutral country, Britain in 1944, was at war with Germany so anything that had to be imported was rationed. As a result lamps were only lit for short periods, or when somebody came to visit, which would be most evenings while the weather held. Candles were therefore much prized but everybody lamented their inferior tallow wax and the fact that you got 'no wear outha dim'. Lackies response was typical.

'Sure what's wrong with fire light' he asked?

'It might not let ye read the Tribune in comfort but its wa-rm and ye won't see the dhusth on the floor, and it doesn't sthop ye telling fine sthories.'

The squeak of the gate heralded Aunt Sarah and Uncle Séameen arriving home. We should have been in bed long since, but were still wide awake with excitement enjoying the fuss everybody was making of us.

Sarah Loftus was a glamorous twenty eight and was born on the Friday following the Easter Rising in 1916. Nobody could deny she was a pretty girl and her cheerful round face showing the remnants of the face power and lipstick she had so carefully applied that morning. Dimples appeared when she smiled, which she often did, because she was blessed with a sunny disposition as well as fine curvaceous body. Her curly hair, may have had a passing acquaintance with a peroxide bottle, and would therefore be a source of scandal in some quarters, Canon Moran, in particular, coming to mind. Her granddaughter, Róisín at the same age bears a remarkable resemblance to her. Having hugged us and kept us clasped to her sides I could smell her evocative 'Evening in Paris' scent, a firm favourite of the single girl during World War 2, and for decades afterwards. It was available in a dinky little cobalt blue bottle from Woolworth's. She started bombarding Lackie with questions wanting all the news, and so it was that we learned what was going on in Claregalway.

Uncle Séameen was a slight man and had his father Tom Loftus's bright blue eyes. He was uneasy around children so I have little memory of him. A thatcher by trade, and at thirty eight, a bachelor by inclination, he was diffident by nature so often has to wait for payments for thatching until after a horse or cattle Fair. Thus it was that the problem of the replacement cow was broached. Winnie pointed out to him that he was no good all at collecting his dues, and was more likely to buy his creditor a drink than press for the debt to be settled. Lackie reminded him of the last pig Market when he returned home with a collie dog on a piece of string in lieu of his thatching fee. The fact that we had no sheep didn't enter the equation. She was named Peggy, and went mad with boredom spending her days herding the piglets and the gander, and creating enough noise to wake the dead. The final straw came when she started eating eggs, so Seanmháthair said she had to go. She was now back in Gorcloonmore with Willie Forde's Aunt, Bid Greally.

I told of our encounter outside earlier, to have Seanmháthair look daggers at Séameen, but Lackie eased the situation and the banter continued as the men sat up to the table to eat the left over potato cakes, and drink the tea now brewed. The soda bread was covered in homemade jam to try to hide the poor quality flour available locally.

In the current circumstances Séameen would need the money by Fair Day to replace the cow. Seanmháthair's contribution was to put her faith in praying for good fortune to shine upon us. This she did with the aid of the little cluster of sun bleached statues on her bedroom window, the Child of Prague, Our Lady of Lourdes, St Anthony, St Vincent de Paul and St Jude. She also mentioned it to the Sacred Heart as she sat in bed saying her rosary before the reflected red light under his picture asking for his intercession with God the Father.

Lackie, more realistically identified a list of debtors with Séameen.

Seanmháthair got a big black cow, at the Cattle Fair, but to a child, in view of what was taken in exchange several days later, it seemed that God and the Saints had the better deal.

Chapter 7; Bedtime in Cloonbiggen

It was ten o'clock, and hours past our bed time when Sarah put us to bed. We were put to sleep head to toe in her single bed, having had our hands and face washed. Although Bridie and I shared a bed at home we were used to a double bed with a bolster between us, so feeling her wriggling legs was very irritating and I was sure I wouldn't sleep, but I was dead to the world before even saying my prayers and woke to hear signs of life at the breakfast table. Aunt Sarah brought us in a bowl of warm water to wash and told us not to hurry because she was busy getting breakfast for Séameen and 'Kerins' to get them on their way back to hay making. Kerins was Martin Kearns a quiet man in his early forties who lived with the family. He had not been home before we went to bed so I had not yet seen him on this visit. He had taken me turf cutting the year before and we had worked in companionable silence for days. I had heard people outside the family calling him 'Martin' but everybody in the family referred to him simply as 'Kerins'. However I liked him and was looking forward to seeing him. Like Lackie, he had a way with children and gave due thought before answering our questions, which we appreciated.

We were not used to washing ourselves, or the luxury of warm water since our Ma was a great believer in strip washes on our half landing, which only had a cold tap so we had a hot bath once a week in a tin bath, me first, then Bridie, then our two year old brother Sean, currently at home in Dublin. Hair washing also warranted hot water, but rinses were with cold water with vinegar added to condition our hair and get the tangles out. While damp, our hair was then combed with a fine tooth comb to remove any lice, and paraffin soaked cotton wool would be applied to any nits clinging to the hair. The latter was hearsay from our friends since we were consistently lice free, but our Ma was obsessed by the thought of lice, and I knew that she had packed the fine tooth comb for Seanmháthair to carry out the ritual. While Bridie scraped a flannel around her face I examined the room. Normally I slept with Seanmháthair in her double bed but this was Bridie's first visit without our mother, so it was decided that we would be happier in Sarah's room, while Sarah shared her mother's.

Sarah's room, which she had shared in childhood with my mother and Aunt May, was big enough to hold a double bed so was comfortably spacious with a single bed sideways on to the window. Facing the door was the wash stand with a blue and white pottery jug and wash basin on top , a towel rail on either side, our clothes neatly folded on the bottom shelf and a small rag rug underfoot, the only covering on the cement floor. The wall facing the window was taken up by an enormous mahogany wardrobe that belonged in a much grander house and which must have been dismantled to fit through the humble portals of its new home. It reeked of mothballs and turf imbued clothes, and was the hanging space for everybody in the house. A small chest of drawers with a mottled mirror on top and painted Dutch blue completed the furniture in the room. The only adornment on the walls was a picture of the Immaculate Heart of Mary at the foot of the bed, with a tiny shelf on which stood a blue glass night light holder.

Sarah had lit a candle remnant when she put us to bed and put it in the holder and that little blue glassed candle had been our only source of light. She had also showed us the white chamber pot under the bed so Bridie and I were now debating whether to use it or traverse the farm yard to the straw pile behind the hen house. Since it was a fine day we set out for the hen house only to find the gander there ahead of us. We eventually found a private enough spot but began to think of our outside water closet in Dublin as five star luxury.

Chapter 8; Language Barriers

When we went back into the house we found Sarah scattering old tea leaves on the floor to damp down the dust and ash while she swept. Two pet hens had come running in when they saw her scattering what they assumed was food and were busily pecking under her feet. Her broom had seen better days and she told us 'John the fear pa', the journeyman and maker and purveyor of handmade rush brooms, would be passing through for the Galway Races so we would get a new one then. The culprit for the broom not reaching its allotted life span was Peggy who had taken to attacking it when anybody tried to sweep. Sarah shooed the hens outside with a 'bad cess to ye' curse and closed over the half door to keep them out. The little table under the window was set out for our breakfast and with a choice of porridge or eggs we both choose eggs. I knew that eating at the big table yesterday had been a special treat and that for the rest of the holidays we would be back to the local tradition of seating and feeding the men first, then the children, followed by the woman of the house. As visitors Bridie and I would eat at the same time as the men, but it would be at our own little table.

Sarah was plaiting my hair when Seanmháthair came in through the backdoor and put a trug full of vegetables on the table in the scullery. Around the farm she always wore long woven skirts with a blouse and cardigan, black woolen stockings and boots or clogs. Then depending on the weather a small shawl crossed over her chest and tucked into her belt on either side, or a well worn mans bawneen jacket. Despite this ensemble people who remember her would say that she somehow always managed to look elegant. Today she was wearing the jacket although it was now pleasantly warm outside. She paused to take a pinch of snuff enquiring about how we had slept, and whether we had enough to eat. Taking two apples from her jacket pocket she gave them a shine on her sleeve and put them on the table telling us to help ourselves. Hanging behind the scullery door was her apron which she now tied around her waist, another use for an old hessian flour sack. Like petrol, and many other commodities, clothing and cloth were on ration, so wasting a coupon on an apron would be foolhardy. Cotton flour sacks were much more highly prized, but were as rare as dinosaurs at that time.

The big pot of unskinned potatoes was already over the fire so she and Sarah set to preparing the vegetables, and began a lengthy conversation in Irish. I couldn't even get the gist of it, but realized that it was a great incentive for a curious child to learn Irish as a second language. No self respecting Dubliner spoke Irish, so De Valera had made it compulsory in national schools, City children regarded it as a curse and a penance, and up to now I had been no exception. My mother spoke Irish, as did most of her friends from Claregalway when they came 'up' to Dublin or were described by those they had left as 'above in Dublin'. This phase buggered up my geography and my sense of direction for years, until I learned Galway and Dublin were on the same latitude and that 'above' and 'below' have meanings which would only confuse a foreigner, or Jackeen for that matter. Roddy Kelly was an exception to the 'as gaeilge' visitors having been brought up in America. The Ma's conversations were never a source of interest to me because I would get the English version when she later relayed it to my father engrossed behind his newspaper. His monosyllabic contributions never interrupted her flow, so if I wanted her to amplify anything of interest to me she would do so without much though, but afterwards giving due consideration to my possibly repeating what I had learned, she would make me promise on pain of the eternal torments of hell not to tell anybody. It was thus I learned about prolapsed wombs, varicose veins, husbands who liked a jar, marital duties, weddings at short notice, and myriad other sources of scandal, without having a clue about what any of it meant.

Of course I told Granny Redmond everything when I went to stay with her on Saturday nights. I knew that this was probably a sin but since I hadn't yet started learning my catechism I wasn't sure which category it fell into, so added an Act of Contrition to my prayers, to appease God, who was, no doubt, looking down on me in sorrow.

Chapter 9; The Staff of Life

Both the hares had been skinned and cut up and Seanmháthair was now rolling them in flour before tossing them into the bacon fat sizzling in a cooking pot which was resting on embers taken from the fire. A jug of water was then poured in, and a bunch of herbs tied with string followed. Sliced onions, carrots, turnips and leeks went in on top. The lid was put and the pot was lifted onto the hook to cook slowly over the fire. Bridie and I watched all of this with great interest. We had a gas cooker at home so cooking was quick and efficient and Ma did not encourage young children to hang around while she was cooking. 'Will ye for God's sake get out from under me feet' was a constant refrain, or, unless there was a hoar frost outside, 'Will ye for God's sake go out and play 'til your dinner's ready'. We did many things for God's sake in our house. We also did a fair amount for Jesus, Mary and Joseph and All the Saints in heaven.

Sarah gathered up the guts and other pieces of hare that had escaped the pot, put them on a small enamel plate, and told us to take them out to the barn cats. Cats were working animals so were not normally fed, never came into the house and did not have names. They were given a saucer of milk when the cows were milked and would normally sit quietly by the milker waiting for the saucer to be filled. Although they were wary of us two black and white cats appeared from behind some bales of straw. We put down the plate and left them to it.

Seanmháthair had started bread making when we went back in the house. The table was floured; a pound of flour was scooped out off the sack and sprinkled with salt and baking soda. The flour was crafted into a volcano shape with a hole created to pour in a cup of buttermilk and then Seanmháthair started mixing it all together with the tips of her fingers. When the gloppy stage was over, she told Bridie and I to wash our hands and that we could do the kneading. No sooner said than done as we squeezed and pounded the life out of the dough. She then patted the dough into a round shape and lightly scored it into quarters to help it rise. Sarah came over to examine our handy work, laughed, and said wryly 'Well 'tis only Faith will get *that* to rise'.

She opened the door to let the two chickens in again to clean up the flour we had scattered on the floor in our enthusiasm. They were also happy to pick the remnants of the dough from between our fingers, saving us another trip to the water trough.

At this point we learned from Sarah what the long conversation in Irish had been about. All the family and the neighbours wanted to see us, but certain niceties had to be observed not to discommode anybody. Other considerations were that the men were out harvesting and the women would be busy cooking for all those helping out, so this meant that our only transport was by bicycle and Sarah had no crossbar so could only take one of us. Having decided that the Qualters in Gortcloonmore, should be our chosen destination the logistics of us getting the two miles down the bog road were discussed and eventually it was agreed that Bridie and I would set out and walk and Sarah would follow on behind on her bike and catch us up. However it soon transpired that our problem was solved with the scrape of the front gate opening and a 'Dia an obair' greeting being called out as Mick Madden, the post man, stuck his head around the door, doffing his official cap, with its Oifig an Phoist gold emblem pinned above its shiny black peak. 'Agus tú féin' responded Seanmháthair.

Mick was held in high regard by local people, and by the gander, who gave him unhampered access from gate to door. Like Lackie, he and his old colleague Pat Tynan were great passers on of news and even greater guarders of secrets. A lot of the old people locally didn't read or write, so not only did they deliver letters from the four corners of the earth, depending on where their brothers and sisters had emigrated to, or where their missionary children were propagating the faith, they often had to read the contents to them as well. Sadder were the times when they had to tell them they had no letter for them. DeValera refusing the Allie's request that April to close the German and Japanese Embassies in Dublin had resulted in an embargo on travel for citizens of Éire, which made letters home a crucial lifeline. Transatlantic letters ceased, leaving people dependent on the telegram, but to send somebody a telegram in wartime was to invite a rise in local mortality rates. I wasn't aware at the time that his official delivery route was Kiltroge townland, not Gortcloonmore. His detours to Cloonbiggen were clandestine and aimed at courting Sarah trying to persuade her to marry him. Mick now had a cup of tea in his hand and with his hat cocked rakishly on the back of his head he listened to our predicament. Before we knew it Bridie was up on his crossbar and I was straddling the back rack on Sarah's bike but not before we were liberally sprinkled with Holy water and blessed with a 'Bail ó Dhia is Mhuire agaibh' by Seanmháthair.

Chapter 10; The Bog Road

There wasn't a soul in sight as we rode out to Gortcloonmore, or **Gort Chluain Mór** as the locals called it, but verges of stacked groigins of turf indicated recent turf turning activity along the road. The bog was a living mosaic of vivid colours, and I recognised some of grasses, rushes, lichens and mosses Kerins had named for me the previous year.

The bogs in Claregalway were located in the townlands of Cloon, Curraghmore, Gortcloonmore, Montiagh and Waterdale. Three people were necessary for a successful days turf cutting so children were in much demand as spreaders. The adult cutter would use his "slean" to cut the sods and throw them up to the two spreaders who would fill a barrow with 10-12 sods, wheel it out to the verge and spread the turf out flat where it was left for a fortnight. After this it was put standing in "groigins" and eventually brought home in carts and creels to be stored for winter. Generally the turf was cut once a year but this was changed to twice a year during the 'Emergency'.

Over the coming years Kerins would show me the variety of birds that made the bog their home; meadow pipits, skylark, curlew, corncrakes and golden plovers, and when they called out in the stillness of the bog he taught me to recognise their cries and calls. We watched iridescent dragonflies, and swallows on the wing and in aerial combat, one being a food source for the other. He also showed me how to find brilliantly coloured jewel beetles in the air filled spaces of bog cotton, and marsh grass hoppers hiding in the sedges and explained to me how the bog grew and regenerated itself. His enthusiasm never lessened, so that even when I grew tired and cantankerous my curiosity became a habit and part of my personality for a lifetime. The only merit star I ever got at school was in recognition of my knowledge of bogs.

It was on this road I had seen the biggest rainbow of my life, and Kerins had to stop me running off to find its end, because I was convinced it ended in Montiagh further in the bog. On cloudless nights the stars in night skies over the bog made you stop in your tracks to wonder at the depth of the blackness as millions of stars sparkled, diminishing in size into infinity.

Gortcloonmore, two miles from the 5mile marker at the Claregalway Crossroads was a long walk to school for its children. It adjoins the Waterdale River on the north end and Montiagh North at its south end. It is mainly low lying but has a mixture of land ranging from good grazing meadows to the left of the road (reflecting the 'Chluain Mór' in its name), to mostly bog and marsh on the right. On the good ground to the left fat Concannon heifers chewing their cud, looked over their stone walls at us. A couple of Kerry Black calves were in the Qualter's field and swallows and housemartins swooped above our heads, and in and around a little cluster of thatched cottages. Suddenly, the bike wobbled and out of nowhere a streak of black and white fur was zig zagging between the wheels herding us into the Qualter farmyard. Thus was I able to confirm Peggy's identity. Sarah obviously found it easier to curse in English, or maybe there were no Irish swear words that gave the same satisfaction. Mick's roar of 'Go dtachta an diabhal tú' was heartfelt but mild by comparison.

Winnie was in the yard in an apron and oversized Wellingtons when we escaped Peggy's clutches. 'May the divil take ye' she shouted after the fast vanishing Peggy, reiterating Mick Madden's curse.

She put down her bucket of water and came forward to meet us. Sarah greeted her with a 'God Bless the work 'as Mick swung Bridie off his bike. He called out to the open doorway 'An bhfuil bean sa chisin'

'Saol fada chu'gat Mick 'Bid replied as she emerged from the doorway wiping her flour covered hands on her apron.

Bid Noone, daughter of Malachy from Cloon, was a smallish woman of sixty three years, and married to Martin Qualter for nearly thirty. Bridie and I got a hug and a 'Ta failte romhat' each, followed by the enquiry 'Ca bhfuil Sean Og'? 'Tá sé abhaile le Mam' was my attempt at a response. 'Cailin maith' said Great-aunt Bid praising me. But before this expectation of my level of understanding and speaking of Irish got out of hand I tried to tell her that I had 'moran' Gailge' which she tut tutted away asking 'An bhfuil ocras ort' then, 'An bhfuil tart ort' followed in quick succession by a 'Cad ba mhaith leat' I realized I had actually understood what she had said so I knew I wouldn't starve or die of thirst, All I had to do now was find the right word for what I wanted, however the only food words that came to mind were aran, prata, ubh, bainne and im. I was wondering if im agus bainne could be used together to make up the word 'buttermilk' Ah, if only learning Irish was that simple. I learned later that 'blathach' was the word for buttermilk, but it was some time before I could string the words 'Ba mhaith liom deoch de bláthach le do thoil' together to ask for it. However Winnie had already rescued me by asking 'Would ye like some 'rid' limonade'?

While Mick bade us goodbye, Sarah took a pot of jam out of her bicycle basket and handed it to Bid, with her mother's compliments. Although the woman of the house always expressed surprise and appreciation at the production of a small token, there would be the expectation that a visitor would not turn up with 'one arm as long as the other' as the saying went, meaning the visitor had turned up bringing nothing. Sarah also produced a small blue conical shaped paper bag, tamped down, and with its top folded and pinched into place, a common way for grocers to sell dry goods. This bag contained tea from my Ma, and was a commodity requiring a ration card so was greeted with much oohing and aahing and blessings being showered on her head. Tea was in very short supply and was used sparingly, anathema to the Irish housewife who was used to having tea on the go all day.

The Qualter's was one of five limewashed houses clustered together in Gortcloonmore. This little townland was once part of the Ascendency Landlord James S Lambert's Estate that had also covered the townlands of Cloughan, Gortadooey, Mullacuttra and part of Waterdale this community had consisted of eleven households on the Griffith Valuation completed a decade after the Famine. There were two Duggan families, the households of Matthias and William and four Feeney's the households of John, Martin, Timothy and William. Jeremiah, John and William Greally are also recorded, as is a lone Mary Noon. My great - great grandparents' Thomas Qualter and Honor Ford completed this little Gortcloonmore community. My great grandparents, Thomas Qualter and Bridget Lenehan, adding seven children to its small population until three of them left to spread their genes.

By the time of the 1911 Census only the Duggan's, Glenane's, Greally's, Feeneys, and Qualters are recorded. Two incomers were the Flaherty's who had married into the Feeneys and Thomas Loftus, my grandfather from Annaghdown who had married my Seanmháthair, Mary Bridget Qualter.

In the 30 years following the establishment of the Irish Land Commission in 1881, the law was changed to restrict the rights of landlords and to encourage the sale of land to tenants. The British Government financed land purchase by tenants by means of loans, incentives and, as a last resort, compulsory purchase. Between 1870 and 1909, it has been estimated that 1.3 million acres of land were transferred to some 400,000 new owners. From a situation in 1870 when 80 per cent of the land was held by less than one per cent of the population, by 1916, nearly 65 per cent of the country was in the hands of owner occupiers.

The sequestering of the Lambert Estate in the early 20th century saw some Gortcloonmore families moving to other townlands to land they got in the division of not only the Lambeth Estate but the adjoining Clanmorris Estate as well.

Family antecedence was of great importance when meeting people, or identifying relations. However, families confusingly and inconsiderately, passed on the same Christian names within the family generation after generation. Suffixes such as **Seán Bawn**, **Seán Ruagh**, **Seán** Dubh or **Seán Óg** were not a lot of help. At least 'Big Bin-e' and 'Little Bin-e' was self explanatory as a form of Bina, Abina or Sabina. Local Bridget's were particularly problematic, derivatives being Bridie, Bridgie, Breege, Breed, Bridgeen, Bid and Delia. Families with several branches like the Greally's were identified as the Casserly-Greally's or the Darby Greally's which wasn't much use to a child ignorant of their antecedents. Likewise married women were known by their own family name so Bid, would never be Bid Qualter, because, although she was married to Martin Qualter, the Qualter's were not her people. She was Bid Noone from Cloon, or Bid Noone of Malachy from Cloon, thereby identifying her 'Clann' as a child of Malachy Noone and Bridget Lenehan, and granddaughter of John Noone and Bridget Higgins, and Cormac Lenehan and Mary Duggan, from Montiagh. As a young child I would not be expected to know 'who my people were' but as the years went by the rote of my ancestors went further and further back depending on the age and memory of the other party. Loftus's, Qualter's, Lenehans, and Duggan's, for half a lifetime, they were all dead people to me, until I developed an interest in genealogy.

The Qualter thatched cottage was a replica of Seanmháthair's except it had four bedrooms and a higher gable end, built so substantially that sixty-five years on it is still standing amidst the ruins of the cottage. My **Seanmháthair** had been born here. She was the sixth of nine children, two of whom were lost to childhood diphtheria and three to emigration, Catherine to New Zealand and Tom and Julia to Indiana.

Settle bed, dresser, tables, stools were all set out in carbon copy positions except that the settle was a newly painted Shamrock green, as was the pendulum clock which began striking its mid day chime and always reminded of Padraic Colum's memorable little poem *The Old Woman of the Road';*

O, to have a little house
To own the hearth and stool and all.
The heaped up sods against the fire
The pile of turf against the wall.
To have a clock with weights and chains
And pendulum swinging up and down,
A dresser filled with shining delph
Speckled and white and blue and brown...

There were several sepia pictures on the wall showing Tom and Julia's families, as well as a turf darkened copy of Millet's Angelus. And on cue, before the chimes had finished, Bid put the jam and tea on the table, next to a round of uncooked soda bread, and wiping her hands on her apron, blessed herself with an 'In ainm an Athair agus an Mhac agus an Spiorad Naomh, Amen, and we all stood and said the Angelus. I was resigned to it being recited in Irish, so we has got as far as 'et verbum caro factum est et habitavit in nobis' before I realized Bid was using the Latin version.

The red lemonade, pronounced 'rid', was produced followed shortly by a dinner of lovely fluffy boiled potatoes the skin cut with a cross and a blob of butter on top and a helping of sweet onions cooked in milk. This was washed down with a glass of buttermilk. Since there were no men coming home to feed, meat was not provided but what we had was satisfying and delicious. As city children we had been used to eating our potatoes skins, but here, with no shortage of home grown potatoes, all the family left their skins which were added to the food to feed the pigs. After a dinner interspersed with constant 'An gabh thu tuilleadh' enquires from Bid, Winnie took Bridie and me out to the small haggard to the left of the house 'to do our business'. There was no territorial gander here but Peggy was lying in wait for us among the misshapen apple trees and determinedly herded us in to the far corner. Winnie picked up a branch and saw her off, cursing Séameen in to hell and out of it for bringing her home.

There were no children of our age in Gortcloonmore, so not having anybody to play with we joined Winnie and Sarah in the yard. They had pulled the well used settle bed outside to open it up and give it a good scrub and replenish the mattress. 'The Settle' was used as seating during the day, and at night could be unhinged outwards and down onto the floor to make a double bed, enclosed on all sides. Its mattress was being replaced with harvested hay removing its winter innards of straw. Tho' prickly, to lie on few occupants bothered to undress and when we children used one it soothed us into a sound harvest filled sleep. With the Galway Races coming up in little more than a fortnight, and visitors, expected, or unexpected, needing a bed for the night, the settle bed would be put to good use in this gregarious lively household. Bridie and I were sent over to Bridget Greally's house to pick up a sack of feathers to replenish the pillows and ubiquitous bolster. Bridget, known as Bid, just to confuse matters, was the daughter of William, and as the last of the four children living at home, had inherited the land from her widowed mother Mary. She was delighted to see us, and in no hurry to let us go. Eventually we headed back with the goose feathers. We didn't see the black and white tornado until it was too late. The sack was ripped from our inert hands, shaken vigorously, and dragged down the road billowing feathers in all directions. Peggy then disappeared as quickly and quietly as she had appeared, leaving us to explain the carnage. The feathers heralded our arrival, reaching home before we did. They also floated back to Bid who on following the trail down to the Qualter's to see what was happening, found two strange little creatures covered from head to toe in goose down. There was a consensus of opinion that her nephew, Willie, would have to let Peggy go.

Chapter 12; An Unusual Day

Late afternoon we set off back to Cloonbiggen, Bridie, on the back of Sarah's bike and me on Winnie's. When we reached home there was no sign of Seanmháthair. The dinner things had not been washed up but inroads had been made in the hare stew. From the amount of unwashed cutlery four people had eaten. Aunt Sarah went in to Seanmháthair's room and found her in bed, an occurrence so unusual that it set Sarah and Winnie into a long whispered conference and an exchange of worried looks. Seanmháthair appeared, and seemed to be her old self, wanting to know our day's doings. At the story of Peggy she sucked her teeth in exasperation, and agreed that she had to go, and like Cromwell, advocated that her destination should be up behind God's back, out in Connemara. Uncle Séameen and Martin Kerins were home just after the Angelus so Sarah took them outside to quiz them about the events of the day, discovering that they, Johnny Qualter and Martin Feeney had broken off from the Concannon haymaking tempted by the thought of hare stew. They had left Seanmháthair to clear up so had not noticed anything out of the ordinary, and were obviously astonished to hear she had taken to her bed. More worried mutterings followed and eventually it was put to Seanmháthair that perhaps she wasn't feeling well and should see the doctor. Winnie quietly removed Bridie and me away from the sound of raised voices by suggesting that we deal with the livestock's end of day needs. I had no idea what all the fuss was about until I gave it some thought. Granda Redmond liked an afternoon nap on a Sunday,' the Gran' never bothered, but the thought of finding either of them in bed, during the day was so alien that I could see why the family might be worried about Seanmháthair's unusual behavior.

Everybody was very subdued after that, and Winnie set off for home before dark and Seanmháthair went to bed early without comment. Sarah got the two of us ready for bed, then we went out to do our business, and in the gloom, came into contact with a group of soldiers carrying rifles. I'd like to be able to say I didn't scream because I wasn't afraid, but it was because I'd lost control of my vocal cords, and if we hadn't been on our return journey I'd have lost control of my bladder as well.

My God, the Germans had landed, and our gas masks were in Dublin was my immediate thought.

'Who goes there' shouted a big culchie voice.

'Is that you Pat Cullinan' said Sarah from the doorway.

'Identify yourself woman' said another voice.

'Shut up ye pack of amadan's ye'll wake me Mother' whispered Sarah.

As they came into the light I recognized Pat, Uncle Mick, Tom and Lackie Qualter, Peter and Michael Glenane, Kerins and Willie Forde,

'What are ye doing? Sarah asked.

'We're on manoeuvres' said Lackie.

'No, I mean *what are ye doing here*'? Said Sarah

'Well we were overcome by a monstrous thirst' and thought that Séameen might have a cure' said Lackie.

'So it's not tea ye'r after' enquired Sarah.

'Mam, if it was the tay we were after, we'd have headed for home' said Willie Forde acerbically.

'Take yourselves of to the barn' said Sarah and to Kerins 'Light a Tilley Lamp and find a bottle of the necessary'

'And watch out for the Excise men' she advised, closing the door, then opening it again momentarily to add '*and* Sergeant Gillespie'.

With not a Pioneer pin in sight they made for the barn as we made for our beds. That was my introduction to a Unit of the Local Defense Force, the cream of Claregalway manhood, our savior's in the event of invasion, English or German. The LDF had evolved from the 1940 Local Security Force (LSF) which had been involved in auxiliary police and internal security work. Following a 'Call to Arms' in June 1940 to defend Éire's neutrality, the Government decided to divide these auxiliary forces into two groups the LDF to the command and control of the Army, now on a defense footing, and the LSF to remain with the Police Force. On the first of January 1941 the LDF became 'An Forca Cosanta Aituil'

Kerins asked Sarah to have us up and ready by eight next morning because he had the use a pony and trap and would take us to Cregboy on his way into Town, and collect us on his homeward journey.

Chapter 13; The Cregboy cousins

Spending the day with the Duggan's was something to look forward to. Aunt Mary had six children at that time, first cousins of our own age. I knew Aunt May would cry when she saw us, and cry when we left, and that Uncle Mick would shake hands with us and tell us we were very welcome, and that it was an honour to have us in the house. There were not many people who thought it was an honour to have children visiting, and even fewer who would take the trouble to tell them so.

Driving along in the pony and trap had been a bumpy ride along the bog road because the wheel span on the trap was narrower by about a foot than the farm carts that had made the ruts in the road, but once the pony felt the surface of the main road under her hooves she got into her stride her high stepping dancing feet tapping out a rhythm on the asphalt. As we passed Bina Lenihan's pub Kerins told us the Moore children were 'down' from Dublin, and like us, would be spending the summer. Further along as we came into Claregalway Village and on the right I recognized Michael Skerret's workshop, Hughes's Shop and Hession's Pub with its 5mile marker outside indicating to weary drovers that there was still a way to go to the monthly fair in Bohermore. As well as the marker there was a cruciform road sign indicating that this was a crossroads and clarifying your four choices. The Church on the left with the school sheltering behind it was identified as the road to Oranmore while the one on the right pointed to Montiagh. The road ahead would take us on to Galway so going straight across at the crossroads with Cregboy townland on the left, I knew that the next house would be Aunt May's, followed by the Casserley's Concannon's Morris's, Quinn's Clancy's and Carr's, while set back on the Cahergowan side of the road was the Cullinan's, all of whom would be sick of the sight of us by the end of the summer.

As if to prove me right there were three children, Tommy, Maureen and Winnie, sitting on the wall waving as we came along. Micheál, a month passed his eighth birthday, had run to tell his Mammy we had arrived. Aunt May came out weeping and wiping her eyes on her apron and was hugging us before we had time to step down from the trap. Bridgie, age ten then came out of the house and bade us welcome. There was no sign of my oldest cousin, Marteen and when I asked Bridgie said he was up the fields harvesting with his Daddy. He was a miniature farmer even then.

Kerins continued on his journey into Galway saying he would be back for us at four o'clock, so we had seven hours of playtime to fill. Sarah had given me a small brown paper wrapped parcel from my mother to give to Aunt May. She opened it and it was no surprise to see an identical packet of tea to Bid Noone's, but further unwrapping disclosed a dozen six inch long Peggy's legs. Nothing to do with the dog you will be glad to hear, but brown toffee flavoured rock. Like many luxuries, sweets were rationed and practically unavailable, parents preferring to use their ration on sugar, so we couldn't believe our eyes I'm sure, like any adult May would have preferred a pound of sugar, but she couldn't deny the delight on the faces of her children as she wrapped two of sticks of rock in a tea towel and broke them into pieces with her rolling pin. She put the pieces on a small plate and passed them around, visitors first. Being well brought up child I declined, and giving Bridie a warning look she declined too, after all, it was our Ma's gift to them, but then childish greed overcame us and we took our share. Access to petrol, tea, and now, sweets would indicate we had a black marketeer in our family, or had a close acquaintanceship with one. I suspected at the time it could be Granny Redmond. She was a bit of a barterer with tradesmen, but her utter contempt for engaging in the 'black market' was well known, so I never did discover who it was.

We were all keen to get out of the house and size each other up to see how we felt about each other. Maureen and Winnie were younger than me at four and two years old, so Bridie fitted in quite nicely between them. Aunt May designated Bridgie as their keeper, which left Mícheál to supervise Tommy and me, who, at five and a half more than capable of getting into trouble. However before we even had time to extricate the remains of the rock from between our teeth we heard the squeak of the garden gate and a 'God Bless all here'. Aunt May raised her eyes to heaven, muttering something under her breath.

Chapter 14; The Radar Station

Mary Casserly lived, with her brother John, in a tiny cottage at the far corner of the Duggan's haggard about a hundred yards back the road, so Kerins would have been fair game for her all seeing eye. For those of you not familiar with the terms 'back the road' or 'over the road' *back* indicated you were going west and *over* that you were heading east. So if you were heading into Galway you were going *back* the road and heading home to Cloonbiggen or all points east you were travelling *over* the road. However not all locals abided by this simple rule so asking for directions could have dire consequences since they also used *back* and *over* in the literal sense.

'Go back the road a bitteen (meaning go back the way you came, not necessarily from the west) take the turn by the Friary and walk back the boreen to the junction, turn right at the *Bean Sí 's* tree and take a few stheps over the road and you're there'. Yea right!

The pony would not have had time to get into a fast enough trot to ensure that he would not be flagged down and interrogated. Mary's antenna could beat the newly invented Radar System which worked using electromagnetic fields any day of the week. Her ability to gauge the range, direction, size and speed of any person, or method of transport, passing her ever open door was legendary.

Her Aunt, Julia Spelman, had previously lived in the 'housheen'. Built by the side of the road it's only window was to the left of the front door so there was no through draft, which meant that depending on the direction of the wind the turf fire either roared up the chimney, wasting turf, or the wind came down the chimney filling the room with smoke so thick it made your eyes water, and you would need a machete to cleave a way through it.

The house consisted of little more than one room with two curtained alcoves for beds and a scullery with a glass aperture. Like all other cottages it had an enormous open hearth, and a few sticks of furniture. The only wall ornamentation was a picture of St Therese of Lisieux, patron saint of consumptives while the deep window ledge housed a ubiquitous collection of small statues and a spindly oxygen and light deprived geranium. Unlike any other cottage in Claregalway it had no backdoor. This was due to some long forgotten dispute when the Duggan's, in an act of kinship, had allowed Julia Spelman's mother, Mary Casserly, to build the house. They had designated a tract of land at the corner of their haggard which had access for a back entrance. Mary declined and the house was built taking a sliver of land from a Duggan field. To give her access to the field would have had all kinds of repercussions so the cottage had neither back door nor windows overlooking the field. The house was right on the side of the main road into Galway, five miles away. Most of the traffic was local, pedestrians, cyclists or the odd horse drawn cart or pony and trap, but they were all flies in her Venus trap. Your chances of escape were not lessened by hail, rain or frost, Mary's door was always open and having neither chick nor child, her life was her own, so to tell her you were in hurry was taken as a personal affront. 'Tis a fine thing then when ye can't sthop to bid the time of day to a neighbour' was a repeated and reproachful refrain. Some years in the future Pat Cullinan would send one of his children, who shall remain nameless, to Hughes's for cigarettes. Obviously the need was great upon him because he said, grimly, 'Don't sthop to talk to Mary Casserly, get back here right away.' To pit a mere child against Mary's determination was folly. When cornered, the poor child blurted out, in desperation 'Me Daddy said I wasn't to talk to ye'. From out of the mouths of babes and suckling's small molehills of offence grow into a mountain of slight.

Mary at thirty three looked older than her years. With hair scraped back in a bun, big horsey teeth and glasses, and no dowry, her prospects of marriage were slim, as were John's. At forty, he worked for the County Council, earning enough to keep both of them, but he had no land, however they were devoted to each other and narry a cross word marred their harmony. With the coming of electricity in the sixties Mary became an avid radio listener which eased the pressure on passersby. Her favourite programme was an RTE 'request' programme and hardly a day went past that she didn't post off a request for a song to be sung for somebody local. She certainly put Claregalway on Radio Éireann's radar.

 'God bless all here' said Mary as she stepped over the doorstep. No Irish here then. Despite the fact that Cregboy townland was in the Gaeltacht the sound of English was much more common in the village then it was back in the bog lands. Mary and Mick Duggan were cousins, his mother Bridget Casserly and Mary's father, John being sister and brother, so Bridie and I were not related by blood, but this made no difference to Mary who clasped us to her turf infused bosom like long lost kith and kin. Bridie and the girls slipped out, but before I was allowed to escape I was questioned about the well being of our Ma and Seán Og. Mary, having caught my Da and Christy on their night at Aunt May's, meant I got off fairly lightly, so Micheál, Tommy and I were off out into the fields within minutes.

Chapter 15; In the name of God

We headed out through the top field full of sugar beet to where Uncle Mick had two horses tackled up to the mowing machine with its deadly blade. The blade was scything huge swaths of hay. We watched as the horses did an expert turn in unison, the horse on the left aligning himself to the next row of uncut hay with the slightest flick of the reins from Uncle Mick. Waving to him, we kept well ahead of the horses and the long cutting blade, and set out on our quest for frogs that would be disturbed by the impending Armageddon.

Startled corncrakes, 'crep crep'd' at us and pheasants took to the air, while rabbits and field mice dashed about as if escaping from a forest fire. We tried to rescue some of the nests taking them to the edge of the field out of harm's way, but we knew it was a lost cause and that the carnage would continue in a few weeks when the threshing machine would annihilate the adjoining fields of wheat.

Frogs however were in short supply, probably because of the dry weather coming up to harvest. However Tommy eventually captured two lovely glistening green ones, at which point we discovered we had brought nothing along to contain them, so he put them in his trousers pocket until we could find something back at the house to put them in.

Home again in time for dinner and we had no opportunity to find a way of stashing them before Aunt May ushered us all up to the table, and started dishing up the food. Bridie's screams brought Aunt May out of the scullery in time to find Tommy scrabbling about under the settle.

'*In the name of God* what's going on in here' asked an exasperated Aunt May?

'Something jumped into me lap' said Bridie

'What are ye up to, you little Spalpeen'? Aunt May said glaring at Tommy, who had his hands behind his back.

'Nothing Mammy' said a guilty looking Tommy

'Then what are ye doing down from the table'

'I don't know Mammy'

'Let me see your hands'

'There's nothing in me hands, Mammy'.

'Tommy Duggan, *let me see your hands,*' insisted Aunt May.

In the mayhem and madness that followed I think she regretted her insistence. When Tommy unclasped his hand, frog number one jumped straight at Aunt May, using her shoulder for a split second as a launching pad before landing on the table. At this point Tommy removed frog number two from his trouser pocket, as much as to say 'Well I might as well be hanged for a sheep as a lamb' or as the Irish version went 'You might as well go to hell with a load as with a bundle' but before he had a chance to ask for clemency, frog number two, squirmed, and escaped from between his bony fingers, joining frog number one in a spectacular jumping competition around the room, both of them ignoring the open door. I didn't know whether to scream or laugh, but looking at Aunt May's face decided to do neither. Maureen, Bridie and Winnie were doing enough screaming for the rest of us. Micheál, blessed with a bit of common sense, was trying, with the aid of a broom, to get them out the door and into the garden. Eventually, he managed it, but did he get a word of thanks, not at all, the blame for the frog fiasco was placed squarely on his eight year old shoulders, since he had been put in charge of keeping Tommy and me out of trouble, ergo, we should never have allowed us to bring the frogs home. Aunt May never met Judge Jeffrey, the hanging judge, but they had a lot in common. Neither of them tolerated not guilty verdicts.

Chapter 16; Dear God in Heaven

Apart from Bridgie we all got out from under Aunt May's feet at her request, and 'In the name of all that's Holy', to allow her to get Uncle Mick's dinner on his plate. We kept well away so had no opportunity to say anything but a hello to him and have him shake our hand and say 'Ye are verra welcome in this house'. Marteen, at twelve, gave us an upward nod of acknowledgement with his chin and looked at Bridie and me from under his straight black Qualter eyebrows as if we'd come from outer space, not Dublin. The afternoon was spent in long games of hide and seek in a farmyard full of brilliant hiding places, We routed spiders, mice, bats, swallows and all manner of God's creatures, in our quest not to be found, and would have played on for hours, only stopping reluctantly when Aunt May called us in for our tea.

At the sight of us, her heartfelt *'Dear God in Heaven'* had to be heard to appreciate the sound of horror in her voice. And looking at us, we were a sight to behold, decades old dust, cobwebs, straw, dung, duck poo, chicken feathers and axle grease adorned our hair, clothes and limbs, while Bridie's and my sandals showed evidence of a couple of encounters with cow pats. The Duggan children at least hadn't committed the latter transgression being barefoot. I discovered that Aunt May was as expert as my Ma when it came to cold water wash downs, and scrubbing children. Afterwards I wasn't sure whether the tingling and redness in my skin was due to her removing the two top layers, or sunburn. Dressed in hand-me-down dresses of Bridgie and Maureen's, Bridie and I, and the mornings welcoming committee, waited for the sound of Kerins and trap to come over the road. Being used to Irish time we didn't hold out much hope for the four o'clock promise, but true to his word the clip clop of hooves could be heard approaching. We heard his voice shouting a greeting to Mary but no break in the pony's rhythm. However he wasn't going to escape that easily. She was outside the front gate before we had a chance to climb into the rig. Seeking news on 'How went his day in town' was like trying to draw hen's teeth because Martin Kearns was a private man, and a polite one, so after a skirmish or two

Mary conceded defeat and with a hupp-hupp and a flick of the reins we were away. As we turned left into the road to Cloonbiggen the vast expanse of sky over the bog on a fine evening was breathtaking, and is a vision of childhood I have taken through life, and never seen replicated until I came across a painting of 'Clouds over the Bog of Allen' by John Skelton. But it's this vista, the smell of new mown hay and jugs of margaritas and marigolds that remain engraved in my memory.

We met up with Delia Holland and her daughter Bridget coming out of the adjacent graveyard. Kerins offered them a lift but Delia declined since they hadn't far to go, being neighbours. Kerins didn't push the invitation when Delia said she was trying to tire Bridget out but he slowed the pony to a walk so that they could keep pace with us. He was a kindly quiet man whom everybody liked, yet very few people called him Martin, referring to him as 'Kerins'or Kearns. Over the next decade he taught me everything there is to know about bogs, but I was seventeen before I learned anything about him.

Bridget, known as Bridie, Holland was a big strapping girl who had problems communicating. Many is the time, in years to come, we would join search parties out looking for her when she escaped Delia's care. For all her problems she never fell into the bog, or wandered far from home, and lived to be a great age. Delia, God rest her, died in 1978. When I was old enough to cycle the Gortcloonmore road alone I set out one evening just as dusk was settling, and was hoping my Guardian Angel would keep me safe from the Bean Sí. I thought my prayers had been in vain because ahead of me I saw an apparition in white, with long streeling hair sitting by the side of the road, keening. I was paralyzed with fright and was about to turn back when I heard voices calling 'Bridgeen, Bridgeen' and saw the flickering light of Peter Greally's lantern in the in the distance as he headed the searching neighbours from Cloonbiggen coming our way. 'You've found her, you've found her' said a relieved Delia. No matter how many times I tried to explain that I had just happened upon her, and that she has scared the living daylights out of me Bin-e, spread the news at the church gate the following Sunday so I was the heroine of the hour. A peculiar feeling for one perpetually in trouble!

Chapter 17; The Doctor calls

Kerins dropped us at the front gate and went off over to Waterdale to return the pony and trap to the Glenane's. Aunt May had parceled up our dirty dresses for me to give to Sarah. We told her, and Seanmháthair, about been scrubbed clean, and the reason we were dressed in hand-me-downs. They both laughed and Seanmháthair said 'Musha what harm would a bit of dirt do ye.' 'Sure ye'r on your holiday' Sarah retorted. They tutted at May's fastidiousness and Bridie and I were hugely relieved to have escaped condemnation, because we knew if it had been our Ma she would have been as one with Aunt May.

When we went outside to see to the stock for the night Aunt Sarah told us that Seanmháthair wasn't feeling well and was restless at night, so she would be using the settle bed not to disturb her. She asked us not to tell anybody. Uncle Séameen and Kerins would know, as would Winnie and Lackie, but until she could persuade her mother to see a doctor she didn't want anybody else worried.

When Winnie arrived with the milk she and Sarah went into Seanmháthair's bedroom to take on the battle of wills to persuade her to see the doctor. Much to their amazement she caved in within minutes.

In conversation later in the evening she admitted she was worried herself because her ankles were very swollen, in fact when she took off her boots they were like balloons. I came from a hardy family where illness was not tolerated. Apart from Granda Redmond's 'touch of bronchitis' earlier in the year, and our fair share of childhood infectious diseases, our elders were great believers in letting nature take its course, so no doctor ever crossed our doorstep, nor did an immunisation needle ever pierce an arm. Seanmháthair saying 'Get the doctor in then' seemed to be letting the side down. She set about getting Winnie to make some chickweed poultices to reduce the ankle swelling, while Sarah searched for something to tear up into rags, bandages being an unknown luxury.

I had only ever seen a doctor when I was sent to the Welfare Clinic on Summerhill by Granny Redmond to get our subsidised Cod Liver Oil and Malt. He wore a white coat, a stethoscope, a mirror on his head and smelled of disinfectant. Dr. Joyce, the Claregalway doctor looked like a farmer, and smelled of turf like everybody else so he couldn't be a real doctor, could he? He and his Gladstone bag went in to Seanmháthair's bedroom. Bridie and I were sent out to find eggs and to look in the clucky hen boxes to see if any of them had hatched any chicks, and with sighs of satisfaction we found a dozen or so newly hatched chicks in one of the boxes, with the last ball of yellow fluff extricating itself from its shell to the sound of its mothers soft crooning sounds of encouragement. In our world of childhood priorities the doctor had long gone before we went back to the house with several eggs and the news of the chicks. Sarah told us that the doctor had left Seanmháthair some medicine because her heart wasn't working too well. She was to take the medicine and have plenty of rest. She set about cooking dinner and when Séameen and Kerins came in told them the news. She needed Winnie Qualter fetched, and for Kerins to go into Town to get the doctor's prescription dispensed, as soon as they had eaten. Winnie arrived at Seameen's bidding and she and Sarah went in to Seanmháthair's room taking her a cup of tea since she hadn't wanted any dinner. After some discussion they came out and told Bridie and me that we would be staying in Gortcloonmore for a few nights until Seanmháthair felt better. We were too young to hide our delight, but old enough to know that all was not well, so it was with mixed feelings that we went into Seanmháthair's bedroom to say goodbye. She squeezed our hands and told us to be good for Bid and to bless ourselves with Holy Water before we set out. She was sitting up in bed with a small crocheted shawl of fine wool around her shoulders, but the memory that is clearest was that she had her hair uncoiled and it was longer than I'd ever imagined. We spent several nights at the Qualter's sharing Winnie's room.

Chapter 18; Lime Washing

Out in Gortcloonmore we spent our days preparing walls for lime wash. Both Bid Greally and Winnie had decided that the houses needed to be spruced up. Bridie and I scrubbed away at the lower walls, first removing flaking old wash, then moss and any other impediments to the new wash adhering to the old coats.

Every family had their own recipe for adding ingredients to achieve this, and prolong the life of the coat, but Bid also added a Reckitt's Dolly Blue Bag to her mixture to add a hint of blue to the brilliant white result. The lime wash itself was caustic so only adults were allowed to use it, although they did so without any safety precautions, apart from having a pail of water standing by for washing off any splashes. The most precarious part of the undertaking were the tall gable ends of the houses, and Winnie did both, going as high as she could go on a handmade twelve rung ladder. Bid press ganged her twenty eight year nephew, Willie, Peggy's reluctant owner, into reaching the last few feet of the highest point. Newly lime washed cottages looked picture postcard perfect and set up a certain amount of envy in neighbours hearts, and strife in marital relationships. Lime washing was regarded as *mans* work but with Winnie and Bid Greally showing such capability, husbands were suggesting that wives should take it on, while wives were making it plain that they had more than enough to do.

Bid Greally was next in line to have the Station Mass said under her roof so the whole house was being lime washed inside and out in anticipation and all the furniture painted to pass the critical appraisal of the flock of parishioners who would attend. To be chosen to have the Mass under her roof was a great honour, an occasion of special hospitality to neighbours and friends, and a time to reunite with seldom seen branches of the family. She had a long list of jobs for Willie to do as soon as harvesting was over to get the yard ship shape and fit to withstand scrutiny. The tradition of the Mass went back to Penal Law days when catholic churches had been destroyed, and priests were on the run in justifiable fear of their lives. Moving from place they gathered people together either at isolated Mass Stones, or in safe houses known as 'stations'. Houses were chosen randomly because secrecy was of prime importance. The Mass became known as a 'station' Mass or more commonly 'the Stations' to put the local Militia off the scent.

When all the painting was finished it looked great. Glancing around the house the only thing with legs that Bid hadn't painted Cardinal red was Peggy. She had painted herself. As Bid's pendulum clock struck the hour I noticed that it too glowed red. Several days of scrubbing and cleaning followed before the actual Station Mass. Bridie and I and several visiting Greally children were commandeered by Willie to guide people into Qualters field to park up their mode of transport. Much more fun than sitting through Canon Moran's Mass. Seanmháthair hadn't attended the Station. However when we went back to Cloonbiggen she was up, and dressed, and cutting an apple pie into slices, anticipating visitors, when we arrived. We were full of news and she was interested to hear it all.

'Wouldn't it be grand if I had children who would lime wash this auld shack' she lamented taking a pinch of snuff. 'Ye'd niver believe I've a son who's a thatcher';

'It must be a full 'tin' year since a ladder was 'lint' on that thatch and sorra a wan cares'.

The latter remark fell on stony ground since Séameen wasn't there to hear it, and Sarah did a lot of muttering under her breath but made no offer to engage in lime washing.

Sarah told us there were another two clutches of chicks so were off out as soon as we had our dinner. There was obviously some discussion about plans for Race Week which would be starting on Monday. My Ma, Da and Sean would be down for the week and would be staying with May. Bridie and I were asked if we wanted to stay on in Gortcloonmore with Bid. To encourage a positive response Winnie pointed out that Seanmháthair could have her bed to herself, which would help her feel better. We would have gone back to Bid's quite happily without the nudge.

Chapter 19; Wives and Daughters

Winnie and Sarah made plans for Saturday's weekly Market Day. This week's market would be big, with everybody needing money for the Races, and entertaining. The races were the social event of the year so it was essential for work on the farm to be reduced to a minimum. Travelling farm hands, who turned up for the harvest on the big farms were nowhere to be found during Race week.

As farmers daughters the only money they earned was what their mothers shared with them from rearing poultry and selling eggs. Unless the family had the means to raise a dowry, daughters fulfilled a role working on the home farm, with no hope of inheritance, keeping house for their unmarried brothers, marrying a widower and looking after his children, or being matched to an old bachelor, provided she was still young enough to bear children. To gain any kind of independence or choice, a daughter had to forsake her home, and travel. For Winnie and Sarah eggs would make a good price this year with them being on ration in the towns and urban areas. A clutch of chicks old enough to leave their mother would also sell well, so they arranged to get a lift to the village and catch the weekly bus into Galway.

The bus was not a place for children, because from the roof down every available space was given over to livestock and produce. The driver was a gregarious and philosophical man whose comments and wisdom were lost in the cacophony of noise from the women who used the journey to catch up with the news and scandal of the day. Even the livestock kept quiet to let the women had their say. The bus kept a steady pace in deference to the baskets of eggs, but the odd pot hole made the bus jump bringing a shower of curses down on the driver's head, some of them to last unto the seventh generation of his progeny.

Sarah had written a list of what they needed to buy or barter. This included Lyle stockings, sugar, tea, and salt and a Baby Powers for Seanmháthair's medicinal needs. When she finished she wrapped our few remaining belongings in brown paper. Bridie and I had travelled in to Cloonbiggen in Willie Forde's horse and cart. He was on his way in to give a hand with the Holland's hay harvest. They would be using the Tumbling Paddy that day which meant every available helper would be needed to get the hay build into ricks. Winnie put Bridie on the back of the bike leaving me to walk to Holland's.

The hay had been raked into rows by the wheelraker a few days before, so now the Tumbling Paddy collected the rows of hay into big piles with a big comb like contraption that formed a cradle. When the cradle was full a lever was thrown forward so that the hay fell out to form the base of the ricks of hay. The rick was then built up to form a half oval shape. This was a job for men and women but called for somebody light, and with a good sense of balance to stand on top of the rick and gather in the hay being thrown up by the pike full. The hay was pulled underfoot and tamped down making a sturdy and firm rick.

The tamping was done in bare feet, so the rick maker often had to be replaced to remove briars and thorns from her feet. The ricks were then tied down with hay súgáun's weighed with stones. The long twists of the súgáun ropes were in the sign of the cross, one stone weighted down each quarter, like a huge baked soda bread, to keep the hay safe until it could be transported home. The workers were on their fifth rick when I turned up.

Delia Holland, Bin-e Greally and Maggie Connell were in the kitchen making tea to bring out to the field. A small mountain of bread and butter was on a tray covered by a clean piece of muslin. Bridget was under surveillance, but seemed happy enough sitting at a small table having her tea. While they worked they too discussed what needed to be bought and sold on Market Day, and how best to ensure that the money for any animals sold at the Fair reached home without too much being wasted on self congratulatory deals by the men folk. The tea was made by pouring hot milk into a white enamel pail, followed by tea leaves in a twist of muslin, sugar, and then hot water. Then the pail was covered, and along with the bread was carried up to the haymakers. A great cheer went up when we appeared as the workers wiped their sweaty, and hayseed covered heads and faces, on various pieces of apparel. It was a magical few hours, so little did I think we would be waking Seanmháthair the same evening a week hence.

Chapter 20; Family reunion

Saturday came and with it the weekly Market Day and the arrival of my parents and Sean. They were coming down by train and catching the market bus from Galway. We were all sitting on Aunt May's wall waiting when the bus chugged and coughed it's way past, as if the laden weight on the way in, had sapped it's strength for the day. We took off after it knowing it would stop by Hession's field at the cross roads. The three sisters got off one after the other, May first, with her lovely Maria Dolorosa face and wearing her country woman's black shawl, then Sarah, in a summer dress and cardigan made to set off her curves blonde, dimpled, powdered, rouged and lipsticked to the nines, and finally my tall, elegant, fine boned mother, Julia, fashionably suited, complete with cloche hat and gloves, a carbon copy of Margaret Lockwood. The Loftus girls were home. A stranger looking at them would be hard put to say that it was the same woman who bore them. My father was one of the last off the bus, carrying Seán. My brother gazed at us as if he had never seen us before in his life, My fastidious mother raked us up and down, as if wishing that she too could deny kinship, because from head to toe Bridie and I were like tinker's children, from our bare feet, scratched skin, and in my case, a plait that hadn't been undone for at least three days. Bridie, who'd had her hair cut, on a whim of my mother's, shortly before the holidays, also showed evidence of neglect. I could see the glint of the loofah in Ma's eye, and an urge to fine comb us to death, and thanked God we would be going back to Bid, who had less demanding standards. Our heads had not seen a nit comb since we left Dublin. Like a lot of Irish mammies, Ma described her children with certain adjectives affixed to our names. Seán was always *my* Seán, I was *that Bernadette Mary*, and Bridie was *poor* Bridie, I think primarily because she had me as a sister.

 Mary Casserly had been left in charge of us while Aunt May was in Town, and was in her element, humming away to her heart's content and showing no signs that she regretted having to relinquish her concierge status for the day. As child minder cum tea maker her reward she would be to hear all the news first hand. She had tea ready for the adults while we children sat on the grass in the garden and had red lemonade and rationed shop bought biscuits as a special treat. Eventually Seán left my father's side and came out to join us. Much to my amazement, he has learned to talk in the three weeks we had been away. For an Irish child not to be talking by the age of two was to be regarded as retarded. When we last saw him he had only got about seven words to see him through his daily needs. They were *'tarry'* which was the imperative form of 'carry me', *'mine'* *'no'* *'ball'* *'wee wee'* *'kaka'* and *'dis'* the latter being any object he was pointing at and wanted. With two attentive sisters anticipating his every whim, he had had no need to extend his vocabulary, but left with a Ma whose nurturing abilities were a bit flaky, he seemed to have learned that talking was less exhausting than having temper tantrums. At two and two months he was quite cute, a little curly headed dote, and the same age as Winnie Duggan. However now that he had got the hang of stringing words together we couldn't shut him up, nor could we play hide and seek with him around because he couldn't grasp the concept that you had to wait to be found, and that you didn't tell the seeker where the hiders were. Winnie on the other hand was a great hider, and being small, and with some help, could get into the most unlikely hiding places. She was also extremely patient and would wait to be found. Earlier in the week Bridgie called us in for our tea, and it was only the empty chair that alerted us to the fact that Winnie was missing.

'Who had seen her last'?

'How long ago'?

Whispered questions, no answers

Who was going to tell Aunt May?

Would Aunt May notice?

Was the Pope Catholic?

However, Aunt May, to give her due, was quite calm when she came in from the scullery and looked at the empty chair. 'No, tea for any of ye until ye find her' was the retort we heard as we went on the search.

'And don't come back without her' was the ultimatum that reached us before we were out of ear shot. And find her we did, and quite quickly. She was fast asleep in a bed of straw in the hen house.

After Mass on Sunday we went to see Seanmháthair who was expecting us, and our Ma and Da and Sean, for dinner. Seanmháthair looked well and the swelling of her ankles had gone down with the prescribed digitalis, and probably aided by her home remedy of chickweed poultices. She bemoaned the fact that she had to pay good money for the doctor's prescription when she had a meadow full of foxglove outside her front door.

Chapter 21; The Galway Races

The days passed with visitor's coming and going, and most of them staying around Claregalway for the week of the Galway Races. Being July there must have been some rain but I only remember sunny days, and since people had to draw water from the wells, it would mean their rainwater stocks were low. Coming, as she did, from a horse breeding family the only child I knew who went to the Galway Races was Maureen Kemple from Lakeview, the townland which started at the church and went back as far as the De Burgo Keep. 'That one was born on a horse' Aunt May used to say, as young Maureen would trot by riding bareback. Little did Aunt May realise she was talking about a future daughter in law. But race goers or not, we all knew the big day of the week was Thursday, a combination of Lady's Day and the Galway Hurdle.

  We had hitched a lift up to Aunt May's and spent the day watching all the unusual traffic passing by heading for Ballybrit and the Race Track. Pony and traps, jaunting carts, and anything on four legs that could pull a cart was pressed into service, so donkeys, jennets, and great farm horses joined the parade. As many people as possible, and with a few more added, to ensure maximum discomfort, were transported, passed us with many greetings and blessings. How they would get home again depended on the Will of God, and the whim of the driver, because by that time drink would be taken, and the chances of the driver and passengers meeting up would be slim. Many a reveller would spend a night in a neighbour's settle bed or barn or, depending on the weather, in somebody's haggard under the stars. In the midst of all this celebration I spied one of the Holland boys cycling over the road.

'I have a message for your Mam' he said to Bridgie taking a grubby folded up piece of paper out of his pocket. The next thing we knew was that Aunt May was up on a bicycle, and away out to Cloonbiggen, closely followed by twelve year old Bobby Holland. Her shouted instructions to Bridgie to tell Mary Casserly to mind us were the only words that crossed her lips. Our initial amazement at seeing Aunt May on a bike with her black shawl thrown over her shoulder was overtaken by a burning curiosity, which matched Mary's, when she came to carry out her duties. Not for her the household chores today. She was 'minding childer', so her place was out on the wall where she would miss nothing. Mary speculated at length about who could be dead, who might have had an accident and who had a baby due. The latter puzzled us, for surely the stork wouldn't deliver a baby at the same time as the Galway Hurdle when there might be nobody home. With no Ravens or Magpies to fuel her speculation we had to await further dispatches. For those of you interested in the portents of birds the saying 'He's in the raven's book' meant that a raven had been heard croaking over the house of somebody who was about to die. Magpie news was more encompassing 'One for sorrow, two for mirth, three for a death and four for a birth'.

Bobby Holland came back an hour or so later to leave a message for my mother to go out to Cloonbiggen when she came home from the races, and that he was on his way out to the Race Course now to try to find Séameen and Kerins. We knew from this that Seanmháthair must be ill, but not a word more could be torn from the messenger, despite Mary's well tried interrogation, and intimidation, techniques. His Mammy had him well trained, and he admitted as much when he tried to placate Mary with a 'Sure she'd have me kilt entirely if I said any more'. Mary took us into the house to say a rosary for Seanmháthair. By now my knees were well calloused on Bid Noone's cement floor, where the rosary was recited every night. I could even do it in Irish, and be trusted to lead the 'Se do bheatha a Mhuire's'and to say the 'Gloir don Athair, but I still got lost half way through the 'Ar nAthair's. She then said the endless Litany before we were released back to sit on the wall. We eventually complained about a lack of sustenance so Mary cut up some cold boiled potatoes and fried them in pork fat with snippet's of bacon, and with that, a plate of bread and butter and cool buttermilk we were happy.

My father and **Seán** arrived in Kemple's pony and trap with the news that Seanmháthair had taken a 'bad turn'. Much to Mary's chagrin while we were praying we had missed Séameen, Kerins and my Ma being transported over the road, and out to Cloonbiggen. Martin Cullinan's wife Molly from across the road in Carrowkeel, came over to sort us out when she heard Aunt May wasn't home. Molly Moran had been a school teacher so was well used order and obedience. She decided Bridie and I would stay the night and that she would take Marteen and Micheál, so saying she and my father pulled the settle bed into the girls room, leaving my mother, father and Seán in Uncle Mick and Aunt May's room, while they could have the boy's room instead of sleeping in the settle as they had on previous nights.

When Uncle Mick and Marteen made their way home from the races they learned the news. After Molly fed them, Mick and my Da were sent on to Cloonbiggen to find out what was happening, with strict instructions to bypass Bina's beckoning pub. She designated Marteen and Micheál to see to the animals, Bridgie to get us washed and ready for bed, and set out to get her son Pat to milk the three cows that were creating a commotion at the field gate that was barring their entrance to their milking stalls. Although we stayed awake for hours talking, it was morning before we heard the news.

Seanmháthair was dead.

Chapter 22; Journey's End

Molly Cullinan and Mary Casserly were still there when we woke up. Molly gathered us together and told us simply that Seanmháthair has died the evening before. We asked endless questions but I remember none of the answers. Molly's skill at teaching different ages in the same class room stood her in good stead now as she dealt with these of us who understood, those of us who only wanted their breakfast, and the littlest two, who in a world of confusion and crying, wanted their breakfast *and* their Mammy's. Mary was as much use as a tit in a trance and kept bursting into tears, bringing lumps to our throats and starting the stinging tears all off again. Molly sent Bridgie over the road to fetch Delia Carr, Mattie and Mary's mother, to tell her the news, and ask her to come and help. Between them they got the house organised, Delia getting the makings of a dinner together and Molly taking over the four youngest, while telling the rest of us to find Uncle Mick and get on with what jobs needed doing.

 Poor Uncle Mick had been up early and doing the work of the woman of the house. He could turn his hand to milking cows, but had lost the knack of letting livestock out, or feeding them, nor had he a notion about where the clucky hens and out layers were. He was nursing his hand having had a run in with the gander, obviously not knowing that when you unbolted his door you stood well back to allow him immediate access to freedom. To stand in his way was folly. He also wasn't used to ordering children about, particularly children overcome with waves of crying if you looked sideways at them, so Marteen took on the job and had us sweeping, stacking, carrying straw and tidying everything in sight in the farmyard. Micheál, the sweeper in chief, complained that the straw carrying should have taken place before the sweeping since it had doubled his workload. For a twelve year old, Marteen Duggan, like his mother, and mine, could quell you with a look, so we heard no more moaning. To give him his due he also had a wonderful smile, we just didn't see it very often.

The only phone in the village was at Hughes' post office, but was no earthly use to us, and Claregalway had no homing pigeon enthusiasts, so we would have to depend on Lackie Qualter, Mick Madden, or somebody coming out from Cloonbiggen for enlightenment. It was Lackie who arrived late morning with all the news. As soon as we saw him, we showered him with tears, so it took some time for us to take in what he was saying. Apparently Seanmháthair had not been feeling well all day, she had difficulty breathing and has passed peacefully away in the early evening. I was old enough to know that death meant forever, and that she wouldn't be coming back, but I couldn't understand why God had taken *her*. Her heart hadn't been working properly, but the rest of her was. Or, perhaps it was the fault of the doctor who didn't wear a white coat and smelt of turf, or me, for not praying enough for her to get better and for abandoning her to go and enjoy myself at the Qualters. Somebody was to blame.

Lackie told Molly that Willy Forde would be up to collect us after dinner to bring us to Seanmháthair's house to say our goodbyes. She would be waked that night, and the Funeral Mass would be the following morning, followed by the burial.

Chapter 23; Waking the Dead

Claregalway graveyard, in the grounds of the Franciscan Friary ruins has been a burial ground for more than seven hundred years, but the Qualter and Loftus families, as relative incomers, had only been using it since the famine years, a mere hundred years before, when the Loftus's came over from Annaghdown, and Seanmháthair's, Qualter family, from Lackagh, seeking tenancies on the Clanmorris and Lambeth Estates in Claregalway. On that day there were several men digging a grave. The weather was overcast so the temperature was comfortable for manual work. I recognised Lackie and Johnny Qualter, Séameen and Kerins, and my Da and Martin Feeney. There were two or three others lolling on the ground, smoking. Family and neighbours all working together to bury my grandmother. A tradition carried on to the present time.

When we reached the house there was only women there. Sarah, May and Winnie Qualter were making tea and preparing food for the wake. The neighbouring women would bring a little something with them, but there would also be men to feed until the potency of Uncle Séameen's poteen was put to the test, curbing their need for food. Being Friday no meat could be eaten but the Montiagh relatives could be counted on to bring fish. Maureen Qualter was also out from Galway, and was disinfecting glasses lent by Bina Lenihan. Bid Noone and my Ma were sitting by the fire, Bid whispering a rosary and my Mother eying up the stylish Maureen, who was her only rival in the glamour stakes, Maureen's only advantage was youth. At twenty three, she was fourteen years younger than my mother, but the Ma could hold her own, and could convince herself, with justification, that her clothes couldn't be bettered for quality or fit.

There was a strange sound coming from Seanmháthair's room. It sounded like a coven of Bean Sí's. Bid explained it was the keening of the Montiagh women. I'd never heard a sound like it before or since. It had an unearthly cadence that you wouldn't want to hear passing a graveyard in the dead of night. According to custom, keening couldn't begin until after the body was prepared and the candles lit lest it attract evil spirits that would take the soul of the departed. Then the Bean-Caointhe, the lead keener began a lament; the other keeners joining in.

When the women came out they joined some other Montiagh women squatting roasting fish over a makeshift wood fire in the yard. Montiagh townlands as the name suggests was 'the home of the turf' and were divided north and south by the Clare River. Montiagh North shared a boundary with Gortcloonmore so you could get there in summer if you trekked through the bog, but nobody lived in Montiagh North any more so the women would have had to cross the River from Montiagh South by ferry, or come out the road from Montiagh South at Claregalway crossroads onto the main road turning at the Friary to come in to Cloonbiggen. The River was a mixed blessing emptying Montiagh North of habitation, leaving it to the turf cutters while providing a bounty of salmon poached by Montiagh South families to supplement their diet and income. Montiagh people were nearly all Duggan's, very insular and self contained, and spoke Irish from choice. Like Aunt May, most of them still wore the Connemara shawl. The click clack of their clogs made a distinctive noise on the stones sounding as if a troupe of Irish dancers were getting ready to do a step dance. Seanmháthair being a Qualter and her mother a Lenehan, were multiply related by marriage, so they had come to pay their respects. Lackie used to say 'Sure dem Duggan's do marry each other and a'te their babies'. Well I don't know about eating their babies, but they certainly inter-married as anybody who tries to untangle their genealogical lines will vouch.

Winnie took us in to say our good-bye's to Seanmháthair and to pray for the repose of her soul. Bid and Bin-e Greally had replaced the Montiagh women in keeping vigil by my grandmother's bed. I should say 'remains' but I didn't yet think of her as a corpse or as the 'remains'. She looked as if she was peacefully sleeping. I knew she was dead, and I knew that death meant that she would not be coming back, but that if God was good, she would be watching over me from Heaven. At this stage I had severe doubts about the goodness of God.

Why had he chosen her to die in the first place? Why so suddenly? Bridgie Duggan and I were having this philosophical discussion out on the front wall, she mournful and sad, me prepared to quarrel with God.

We were both very disappointed in God, and felt cheated that he had taken our grandmother, when there were old people in the locality who couldn't do a hands turn for themselves, who would love to go to Heaven.

Seanmháthair's bedroom was lit only by candles, blessed over the years, at the Mission for just such an occasion. All her earthly possessions were put away, apart from her five little statues on the windowsill. The red lamp in front of the picture of the Sacred Heart was alight and gave a warm glow to the room. Seanmháthair was laid out long and straight on her marital bed. Everything in the room was white apart from her brown shroud. The bed linen was of dowry quality with a lace trimmed pillowcase under her head, a lace made bed cover that must have taken forever to make, and a linen sheet covering her as far as her waist, leaving her clasped hands entwined with her rosary beads on view. On her bosom lay the front half of her St Francis scapular with the strings going her head to join the back piece half way down her back. Her hair was dressed into a long plait and came over her left shoulder. We all touched her hand which felt dry and cold and said 'Rest in Peace', which brought floods of tears again. Every time I tried to talk, my voice would quaver, and the tears would well up. I tried to keep well away from Bridgie for the rest of the afternoon, because like her mother, Aunt May, when it came to crying at happy events or sad events, they could cry for Ireland, and the puffiness of their eyes on this occasion bore witness to the fact.

'*Jesus Christ*' said my mother, Julia, leaping up, as a car pulled up outside. '*It's the Canon*'. In my five and a half years I had never seen my Ma move with such speed and alacrity. She grabbed a startled **Seán** under one arm, Bridie by the scruff of the neck, while expertly manoeuvring me in front of her with the toe of her shoe. From the utterance of the sinful blasphemy, to bolting Séameen's bedroom door behind us, can't have taken more than five seconds. Canon Moran still hadn't set foot over the front door, leaving her sufficient time to instill a warning of instant death, and eternal damnation in the fires of hell, to the first one of us to make a sound.

To ensure **Seán**'s compliance she put her hand over his mouth, Bridie and I only got 'The Look'. The door was made of solid oak planks with little shafts of light from the glow of the fire showing through. Ma had to hold **Seán** so I was delegated to survey the scene in the other room, and give a whispered commentary. Unfortunately I could only hear muted voices, and the only view I has of the Canon was his left foot. Ma behaved as if this was my fault. Her rouge became superfluous as her cheeks glowed with rage. I suddenly realised from the rhythm of the voices that the Rosary was being said. When I told her, what came out of her mouth wasn't a prayer. The following de Profundis and Litany for the Dead seemed endless, enclosed, as we were, in a room with a deranged mother.

  Canon Patrick Moran, known as 'Pa' behind his back was a native of Castlebar. The Claregalway Parish priest since 1915 he was feared and loathed by a fair number of his parishioners. To find my mother numbered among them was astonishing, after all she had been in Dublin for a good eight years. What had she done to incur his wrath? I couldn't wait to get out of the room to find out from somebody. I may have been young, but I wasn't foolhardy enough to ask *her*, particularly not at this moment in time. **Seán** started to get restless so got 'The Look' and a shake, and as he opened his mouth to protest, a cajoling quietly sung nursery rhyme.

'I want to do a wee-wee' said he, removing Ma's hand from his mouth, long enough to utter the words. Ma looked at me and whispered 'po'. I looked everywhere; under both beds, in, and under the chest of drawers, wash stand, and even under the pillows, but it seemed neither Uncle Séameen or Kerins has any need for a chamber pot or a jug and wash basin for that matter. I looked around for a container; any container and the only thing I could find on the bottom shelf of the wash stand were two pairs of well polished Sunday shoes.

Somebody would be going to the funeral with a damp foot.

The Angelus bell was tolling as we passed Claregalway Church on our way back to Aunt May's. We met a fair bit of traffic coming from the races, and made peoples journey home longer, as neighbours and friends stopped in the middle of the road, to offer condolences and to say they would be along to Cloonbiggen later. Willie Forde had been pressed into service again but this time we had Aunt May and Winnie Qualter with us and we were minus Seán who had stayed with Ma. Sarah, my Ma, Bin-e Greally, Maggie Connell and Delia Holland would do the *waking,* while Aunt May would see to her own, and Winnie would stay the night and see to us.

Poor Uncle Mick looked relieved to see us, and even welcomed his own wife home with a 'Ye'r welcome, 'Verra welcome, all of ye', 'Verra verra welcome'. He'd had a bad day, gouged by the gander, a bucket of milk kicked over by a bolshi cow who objected to an unfamiliar milker, driven to distraction by Mary Casserly, bossed about by Molly Cullinan finally suffering self mutilation as he had attempted his weekly shave as a sign of respect for the occasion. 'Musha, will ye get out from under me feet' was the Bean a Ti's retort as he tried to unload his tale of woe.

We took this as fair warning that the' *ye',* in this instance, was plural. Always hard to tell in Galway since it was used for both singular and plural, while in the Dublin vernacular the plural was always *youze or yiz* neither of which ever crossed my lips. Sr. Monica our elocution teacher would have seen to that. Her favourite saying, over the next eight years of having a 'gurrier' accent knocked out of me, and my fellow scholars was, 'You may come from Summerhill, but by the time you leave North

William Street School you will sound as if you were born in Foxrock'. Note three *you* plurals. For those of you not familiar with Summerhill and Foxrock, Summerhill was an Inner City tenement ridden area, and Foxrock a salubrious leafy suburb.

It was beginning to rain so we all headed for the hay barn. Mícheál , Bridgie, Tommy and I held a post mortem on the day's events while the little ones listened. Marteen, ever the responsible one, found some tackle to clean. The first item on the agenda was my Ma's behavior. We rolled around and screamed with laughter taking turns trying to beat her speed record. Micheál measured out the distance using a handle from an old hatchet as the entrance to Séameen's bedroom door. Of course to lend authenticity to the scene, we all had to repeat her taking the Lord's name in vain. Following a discussion on this point of Canon Law, we decided that it was her sin, not ours for having to repeat it. Bridgie's suggestion that blessing ourselves when we said it would make it all right was rejected out of hand, because it would slow down the initial sprint, however bowing our heads in respect was allowed. Tommy Duggan won the game so often that the rest of us had to concede defeat.

We then took to speculating on what kind of sin she might have committed to have made her so afraid of the Canon. The only one of us who knew the Ten Commandments was Micheál, but he could only remember them by rote so had to repeat the whole lot each time we reached a new one. Stealing and murder we rejected out of hand, and four of them we didn't understand. We knew she went to Mass on Holy Days and the Sabbath, so that was another one accounted for, and I was able to assure them that the only statue in our house in Dublin was Blessed Martin de Porres, and while he might be a foreign black saint in the making, he wasn't a foreign God, which cleared her of breaking the First Commandment. That left us with 'Thou shalt not take the name of the Lord thy God in vain', or 'Honour thy father and thy mother.' On reflection we agreed that while she frequently broke the former, she wouldn't have broken either in Canon Moran presence.

'She was called from the pulpit' a little voice piped up. We all looked in astonishment at Maureen Duggan, who was delighted to be the centre of attention for once. To be 'called from the pulpit', or chastised by the priest in public, which was what actually took place, was a terrible disgrace and remembered in family annals for generations. To say we were shocked, horrified, awestruck, was an understatement, but to have discovered this family secret also filled us with immense glee, and an urge to hug each other in smug satisfaction knowing a family grownup had feet of clay.

'For what' I asked. 'Don't know' said Maureen.

It transpired that Maureen had overheard Bid Noone giving the Montiagh women this explanation to explain my mother's extraordinary behaviour. Age four, the rest of the conversion was over her head, so we didn't know whether to praise her, or shake her. This took us back to re-examining the Ten Commandments but now asking Marteen for an explanation of the ones we didn't understand. His sage advice was that it was more likely to be one of the Seven Deadly Sins that would get you called. At this juncture, and to add to our frustration, he went back to the house without telling us what the Seven Deadly Sins were.

It had been raining for some time now and the barn was getting gloomy. We had heard Aunt May putting the stock in for the night so knew we would soon be called in for supper. For a couple of hours we had hardly given Seanmháthair a thought and little did my mother know what grand diversion she had provided.

Chapter 25; The Jaunting Car

The morning of the funeral Uncle Mick and Marteen has been up early to scrub out the farm cart, and the horse was now between the shafts and impatient to be off. Aunt May had the milking done and the livestock seen to, and Winnie Qualter had us fed, and dressed in our Sunday best. Bridie, Maureen and Winnie Duggan were being left with Kate Murphy; Molly Cullinan's live in help, and were none too happy, but were being bribed with a promise of sweets

When we got to the road into Cloonbiggen it was a quagmire from the heavy overnight rain, however the ruts in the road and the span of our cart wheels were as one, so we made it to the house, and into the yard without too much trouble. Seanmháthair was in her coffin with the lid off providing one last opportunity for friends and neighbours to view the deceased. In families with a small dwelling the body would be placed in a coffin, and depending on the weather, would be brought outside the house. There, the open coffin would be laid across some chairs to allow the mourners to file by and pay their last respects.

We were told by my Ma to say 'Goodbye' and 'Ar Dheis de go anam naoife'. As I touched her cold rosary bound hands for the last time I felt a deep sense of loss realizing I was never going to see her again dead or alive. She had never been a demonstrative grandmother, but she always showed a warm interest in our day and never condemned our mischief. We all had a little weep and Tommy and I went outside to get away from Bridgie who was sobbing her heart out. We sat on the wall intent on keeping out of trouble and watched in absolute astonishment as a jaunting car and a high stepping pony came struggling down the boreen, the jaunting car swaying from side to side like a cork in water its wheel span being too narrow to ride the ruts.

Questions rose in both our minds, but all we did was look at each other, I raised my eyebrows, he shrugged his shoulders. We watched as more carts arrived, and noticed nobody else was stupid enough to bring a pony and trap, or a jaunting car down, a claggy bog road.   Then I noticed an uninvited guest among a line of restless horses. Weaving in and out through their legs was a familiar black and white shape, red tail swishing; Peggy had come to the funeral. Tommy had never seen her, only hearing of her exploits, so he whistled her over, and patted the wall beside him, and up she jumped and sat quietly between us.

The waiting men took their caps off as Seanmháthair's coffin was manoeuvred through the doorway. Carrying it were Séameen and Kerins, my Da and Uncle Mick, and at the back Martin Qualter, Seanmháthair's brother and his son Tom. The coffin was raised up on the jaunting car and strapped on. The pony set off for the Church, and we all prepared to follow, however with the first turn of the wheels the coffin started to slide, and despite being adjusted it continued to lurch from side to side, every step foretelling disaster. I don't know which of us started laughing first, but Tommy Duggan and I were soon consumed by rippling waves of hysteria that kept surging up past our vocal cords until we were whooping and bent over with mirth. In the midst of this madness I saw we were being observed, and given 'The Basilisk Glare' by our respective mother's.

Our laughter was infectious and some of the onlookers began to smile and enjoy a bit of craic. Peggy began to dance around and bark with excitement. To the question, 'whattotalfeckingejjit' thought this was a good idea', were several suggestions, denied by the accused, a red faced Uncle Séameen. Nothing short of a good slapping or a bucket of cold water over our heads was going to stop Tommy and me. It was I who got my legs skelped *and* a bite from a manic Peggy for good measure. Her incisor marks are still on my thigh to this day. Peggy got the bucket of water to calm her down, and Tommy escaped his mother's clutches, and managed to keep a low profile until the end of the day.

I remember nothing more about the transportation of the coffin or the Funeral Mass; perhaps I wasn't allowed to go. However I do remember the burial because I knew we had no more to do for her and that she was now in God's hands. Lackie Qualter let me sit on the nearby wall and watch as he and his brothers filled in the grave. Martin Feeney kept me company telling me he had helped dig the grave.

'You know, he said 'the last one in the grave was Tom, your Seanathair'

'Nye on eleven years he's been in.' 'Nothing but a skellington now, but begod there was a fine piece of cloth in that suit of his'

'Ye'd get good wear out of it yet 'said the philosopher. I looked at his Aran jumper and corduroy trousers and wondered if he'd been tempted. 'It's hard to believe she's dead' said he, taking off his cap to say a prayer, as the floral tokens were being placed on the filled in grave. 'Well, bejapers, I *hope* there's no mistake' said Lackie wiping his brow, 'We've just shovelled a half a ton of earth on top of the poor woman'.

And so, 'saol seo go dti an saol eile', my grandmother was buried beneath the turf, and endless sky. For many years I thought of her as an old Irish country woman who had never travelled further than Galway, five miles away, and who only left the bog to go to Mass or confession. Imagine my surprise when I found out how wrong I had been.

She turned out to be quite an enigma.

My father caught the milk train back to Dublin that night, leaving my Ma and Seán down for another week. It took some days, and a chance remark from Bid Noone, to learn that Ma would be cutting short our holiday for the convenience of us all travelling back together.

'Don't worry' said Bid, 'We'll work on it.'

Three weeks still to go before school started, was three weeks 'under my mother's feet' and if Christmas and Easter holidays were anything to go by, was not be contemplated as an experience to look forward to.

My Ma of course realised this herself and was not adverse to a little persuasion. God bless the person, whoever it was, who came up with the idea of Winnie Qualter coming up to Dublin to 'give the Ma a hand'? Bridie and I were ecstatic at the thought, and set about convincing an initially reluctant Winnie that we would have a grand time. At twenty two she had never been out of Galway, except to go on Pilgrimages to Knock and Croagh Patrick. The occasional Legion of Mary excursion into Salthill or collecting seaweed at Maree was the only time she had seen the sea, so going to the metropolis was a huge undertaking, and might involve taking her life in her hands what with robbers, white slavers, unruly men and getting lost. Ma pointed out caustically that it was Dublin we were going to, not Istanbul. Only when my exasperated mother assured her that Istanbul was nowhere near Dublin was Winnie's mind set at rest.

A few days later we were packed and ready to go, Winnie wearing her good coat, best headscarf, Miraculous Medal, festooned in scapulars drenched in Holy Water and carrying a small suitcase circled by an old belt to keep it closed since the locks had no key, so the clasps sprung open at the slightest provocation. We were in heaps of time for the mid morning train but knew we had to stop at the Duggan's and Mary Casserly's to say our goodbyes. We had already bid tearful goodbyes to everybody in Gortcloonmore the evening before, and with a 'Go mbeire muid beo ar an am seo aris' Bid hugged us and let us go on our way. In Cloonbiggen we had started our departure with more tears from Sarah, and Delia Holland. Sarah gave me a small package saying it was a small token of Seanmháthair's she would like me to have. I was relieved when Kerins turned up with Glenane's pony and trap to take us on our way. We all climbed in. Bridie Holland included herself in the passengers, and took some dislodging before we were able to set off. Kerins was the bearer of the news that Peggy was now over in Waterdale with the Glenane's who had a fine flock of sheep, and was going to be given a chance to do the job she was bred for. However, they were only willing to take her if she came with her license, so Séameen was going to have to take the trouble to find Guard Kavanagh and purchase one, something he should have done the day he took possession of her.

The Duggan children were all out on the wall, Marteen among them, as we trotted through the crossroads. Aunt May came out to join them, shortly followed by Mary Casserly running down from her sentinel post as she heard the commotion. Everybody cried, some discretely, some as it there was no tomorrow. 'Suffering Jesus, will you get us on our way' muttered my Ma to Kerins. Was there no end to this woman's blasphemy? Kerins stood up in the trap and taking a bag from his pocket tossed the contents up in the air as if it was a wedding grush. There were shrieks of delight as the children realised it was raining toffees, and without more ado, he clicked his teeth and we were trotting away to the sound of fading 'Goodbyes and 'Slán agus Beannacht libh.

The summer children were going home.

Chapter 27; Uncovering Dublin

Winnie had never been on a train before so her excitement was infectious. It was the age of steam so when the driver released the whistle Winnie jumped two feet in the air with fright. Normally we fell asleep on the journey but as we went through Athenry, Ballinasloe, Athlone, Tullamore and across the Curragh of Kildare Winnie had us looking at different breeds of cattle and sheep, the quality of the land, and what could be best grown on it, so that in no time at all we were in Kingsbridge Station and spied my father waiting at the barrier.

For convenience we took a Hackney cab home. Granny Redmond had been in to tidy up, and cook a stew but hadn't removed evidence that half a bottle of poteen, courtesy of Séameen, had been consumed during the week. My mother gave the bottle 'The Look', so my father removed it from view and with a sense of occasion rubbed his hands together saying 'How about chips'? Shop bought chips were a rare treat so the Ma cheered up considerably and put the stew away for next day's dinner. Ma, with her pre nuptial Domestic Science training, said 'We'll eat the casserole tomorrow'. I smiled to myself when I remembered the Grans response when I'd asked her one day if we were having a casserole. 'Casserole my arse', she'd responded, 'its scrag end Irish stew'. Da counted out some money and told me to go down to Summerhill and get six 'singles'. In Italian chipper parlance a single was a portion of chips, and a 'one and one' was cod and chips. Ma suggested that Winnie go with me, but I didn't want Mario to be the first Dubliner Winnie met. Not that by any stretch of the imagination could Mario Staffieri be mistaken for a Dubliner. He was a balding roly poly Italian from Casalattico, with a fiery temper. His black curly hair had now receded to a halo along the base of his skull. He manned the fish and chip fryers while his younger sister Maria served the customers. The continual barrage of insults he aimed at her was like water off a ducks back. Her serene smile and politeness never wavered, and the regular offers from local men, *and women*, to give Mario 'a good going over', was always met with a smile and 'He a gooda man'. 'He a noa means it'. Why did customers continue to frequent the shop? Because Mario made the best chips in Dublin, and his battered fish drew customers from Drumcondra to Marino. I ran home with our 'single's' to find the Da frying eggs we had brought back from Cloonbiggen, and Winnie buttering bread with Bid's churned butter. It was a meal to remember.

The next two weeks saw Winnie's confidence blossoming. Getting around Dublin is easy enough once you've learned to take your bearings from O'Connell Street, Dublin's main street, and the terminus for buses coming in from all the suburbs. One of the widest streets in Europe, a legacy of the 1751 Wider Streets Commission, one end of the Street stops at the bridge crossing the Liffey and is overlooked by the sumptuous monument to Daniel O'Connell, while at the other end, the Rotunda Maternity Hospital, with Parnell's declamatory bronze monument in the middle of the Street outside forms the other boundary. This monument identifies the traversing street as Parnell Street, which became Summerhill where a left turn at Upper Rutland Street saw us home.

Normally we had to test the barometer of my mother's moods on a daily basis but during Winnie's stay she was cheerful, easy to live with, and generosity personified having two frocks made for Winnie and crimped her hair so that she no longer looked as if she was 'Up for the Day', the latter being the derogatory way the average Dubliner described a country bumpkin, or *culchie*. The 'Up for the day' jibe was derived from the fact that most *culchie's* only came to Dublin on an excursion train to attend Croke Park for All Ireland GAA Football and Hurling matches, returning home the same day. Ma took pleasure in Winnie's delight, and although she mostly didn't accompany us, trusting me to know my way, she gave us spending money and fares to take us to the Zoo, Botanical Gardens, the Phoenix Park, Dollymount Strand and up Nelson Pillar. We uncovered a Dublin for a Winnie mad for adventure. On wet days we left Seán with Gran and went to the pictures, or a show at the Royal. On her last day Granda Redmond took us on the Liffey boarding his old tug where he had been a Lighterman and one of its designated firemen. The tug smelled of axle grease, and tar from newly treated ropes, while the air was a heady mixture of hops from Guinness's Brewery and the unique aroma of Liffey water.

But what Winnie really enjoyed was sitting out on our front steps with the neighbours in the evening sun, keeping an eye on their playing children. My mother never engaged in this activity. Being an in-comer (or blow-in), with only four years credentials locally, she had never felt at ease with born and bred Dubliner's. Granny Redmond used to say

'It's nothing to do with her being bread and buttered here'

'Julia Loftus thinks she's too good for Upper Rutland Street'.

Or, an observation that was equally valid,

'That woman would be a lot happier if she had married a man who could give her a lady's maid and a nursery nurse, to be at her beck and call'. An observation of my own would be that Ma would be a lot happier if she has a husband who spent less time at the ITGWU at Liberty Hall.

Julia Byrne, aka Granny Redmond, and a sixth generation Dubliner from the Liberties, only has one thing in common with her daughter in law Julia Redmond, nee Loftus, they shared the same name, although in years to come they would share the same grave. When it was time for Winnie to go home we were bereft, and I looked forward to going back to school.

Winter and spring of 1945 passed and the Emergency continued with tighter rationing, censorship, internment and more hardship. Roddy Kelly, a friend of my mother from Loughgeorge used to arrive laden with produce. His father Malachi, and Seanmháthair, had some connection lost in time as is Roddy's relationship with my mother. We also used to go over to tea in Dundrum with Delia Lenihan, Bina's sister. She was married to John Moore, and the mother of the other 'summer children', John, Kathleen and Marie. When Delia and the Ma had come to Dublin, Delia came to train as a Nurse and my mother to do a Domestic Science Course with the Presentation Nuns.

During the swapping of news on these occasions I learned that Sarah had married Mick Madden, the postman, had a new baby, and was living in Loughgeorge. My initial reaction to the news was totally self centered, 'How was this going to affect my summer holidays'? I waited for Ma to tell Da the news, so that I could then legitimately broach the question. For once in his life he was showing an interest in the conversation, and asked the all important question 'So, who's having the kids? Bridie glanced sideways at each other and I waited for the answer with bated breath through what seemed like an endless pause, while Ma replenished her tea, and cut up fingers of toast for Seán, 'Bid Noone's offered 'she said. We made no expressions of delight, because we knew Ma would hold the threat of us *not going* over our heads, every time we annoyed her between then, and the day of departure. Also, I had to get her in a good enough mood at some point before asking her why she had been called from the pulpit. Winnie hadn't known about the calling, never mind the reason, so had been of no earthly use, refusing to ask Ma because it would be 'an ignorant thing to do'. What child worries about the niceties of polite society? I *needed* to know. How could I admit defeat to my Duggan cousins?

By June the War in Europe was over but rationing and shortages appeared to be worse. It seemed we were being punished for Éire's neutral position and De Valera's intransient stance over the past five years. When he offered his condolences to the German Ambassador on Hitler's death the repercussions from America and Britain were noticeable, but not acknowledged, however our exports were taxed out of the water, and our imports practically came to a standstill. We were persona non gratis in diplomatic circles, so unless we could produce what we needed within the twenty six counties, we went without.

Granda Redmond, a Larkinite by political persuasion, cursed De Valera as the Devil's spawn, who should be deported to hell if possible, or, or if not, to whatever country his putative father came from. Travel became difficult as buses and train timetables were reduced. Gas usage was rationed and was only available between certain hours so the Glimmer Man's rounds became more frequent. It was illegal to try to use the residual gas in the pipes, so children would be sent out on a 'recce' to watch out for the Inspector from the Alliance and Dublin Gas company. I don't actually remember The Glimmer Man ever visiting anybody, but he was our childhood Bogey Man. 'The Glimmer Man will get you if you don't watch out'. No Black Market petrol this year, but plans were afoot to use the Da's influence in the Irish Transport and General Workers Union, his second home, first priority and the cause of most of my parents marital rows. A coach would be going to Galway for some kind of regional meeting the beginning of July, so he set out to inveigle two seats for Bridie and me. The problem of getting us back to Dublin would be considered in due course.

The coach set off from Liberty Hall and the journey was a nightmare. A vehicle full drunken delegates was no place for children. I thought that sitting near the rear would keep us out of harm's way, but had not been aware that the back seat would be used for crates of porter. What we gained in shortened travel time we paid for in discomfort from the stench of porter being liberally passed around. I wondered how, in an era of dire shortages, Guinness seemed to be freely available but I suppose the fact that it was 'home brewed' had something to do with it. Our rendezvous point was Bina's pub, but if the blathered, and full bladdered TGU men had thoughts of relieving themselves in comfort; they were in for a big surprise. 'Doing your business' at Bina's was an outdoor pursuit. As we pulled into Bina's front yard in the shadow of the Friary Ruins I saw the Qualter's horse and cart over in a quiet corner, the horse chewing contentedly on a nose bag full of hay.

Chapter 29; Bina's

At a few minutes past three in the afternoon the snug was empty.

'Jasus, is it the Holy Hour or wah' said one of the delegates

'No' said a cultured voice from under the counter.

'I can serve a Bona Fide traveller between two thirty and three thirty any day of the week' said Bina popping up into view. The look of astonishment on the delegate's face when he put the voice to the Wreck of the Hesperus standing before him was a joy to behold. Bina was a Celt and woman in her prime. Good bone structure and a fine square jaw made her an attractive woman, but nobody could ever accuse Sabina Lenihan of making the best of herself. From her prematurely greying sandy hair, to her men's boots she had to be seen to be believed. Her abundant hair was scraped back in a bun with escaped tendrils latched behind her ears, her spectacles were so misty it was a miracle she could see out of them, and her wrap around apron so encrusted with grime it could stand up of its own accord. But by far the most memorable thing about Bina was the eternal cigarette smoldering in the corner of her mouth.

The cigarette was never removed. When it reached butt status a new one was lit from the dying ember. The cigarette was never flicked, so it was fascinating to watch the ash getting longer and longer while anticipating into whose drink it would fall.

Bina called out to Bridie and me to make our way to the kitchen which we did, carrying a suitcase between us. I loved the smell of Bina's snug a mixture of peat, porter, damp and ammonia. To a city child they were foreign but somehow comforting and familiar. Winnie and Uncle Martin were sitting drinking tea. Missing was 'Aunt Kate', Bina's mother, Catherine, a Kelly from Waterdale, who had died aged eighty two that March. I still half expected to see her sitting by the hearth smoking her clay dúidin. We soon took our leave with Winnie driving. Martin's rheumaticky hands showing he could no longer control a young horse. With a click of her teeth to the horse, Winnie gathered the reins, and with a left turn out of the Pub yard, and a right at the nearby Friary Ruins, we were back on the Bog Road. She pulled over by the graveyard wall.

'Let's tell Seanmháthair you're back' she said.

There was no grave marker but I knew where the grave was, and even if I had forgotten I would have recognised the jug of marigolds and margarita's from her garden. The plot had been weeded, and the edges trimmed.

'It looks as if Kerins has been busy' said Winnie.

We said a quick prayer for the repose of Seanmháthair's soul and went over to say a prayer at Kate's grave, then with a

'Let's be on our way before the rain comes down' from Uncle Martin we set off for Gortcloonmore with him drawing on his pipe.

Uncle Martin was an expert weather forecaster. He neither knew nor cared what cloud formations were called. His expertise was in watching nature. Dandelions and chickweed closing their leaves, low flying sparrows, chickens making for their roosts, frogs croaking in the bog and the cows with their tails to the wind. On the other hand my Uncle Billy, Granny Redmond's brother, a little man of esoteric knowledge, had taught me four essential Latin words to describe clouds, Cumbus, Cirrus, Stratus and Nimbus. I learned that by standing with one's back to the wind and observing the movement of the clouds, it is possible to determine whether the weather would improve or deteriorate. If the clouds are moving from the right, a low-pressure area has passed and the weather will improve; if from the left, a low pressure area was arriving and the weather would deteriorate.

'This is known as the 'crossed-winds' he told me which I misheard as cross winds and which made perfect sense to a child.

That day all I saw was a cumbus cloud formation with the sun appearing and disappearing between them, and no nimbus rain clouds to speak of, but Uncle Martin forecast rain and worse.

'Wouldn't be surprised if we had thunder before the night is out' he mused as we recommenced our journey.

We hailed Michael Madden cutting turf in the distance.

'Only an eejit would slane the turf with the swallows flying that low' he opined squirting a jet of tobacco stained spit from the corner of his mouth.

Bina did good business out of the delegates before sending them on their way to their hotel in Salthill. I never did discover if any of them had ventured to eat anything during their stopover. To consume anything on the premises was to take your life in your hands.

Chapter 30; Gods bounty

'Cen chaoi 'bhfuil tu', 'Cen chaoi 'bhfuil tu? repeated Bid as she hurried out to meet us followed by a 'Come in', 'Come in'.

Bridie and I were about to step over the doorstep when the first fat drop of rain in a week fell in the yard. Uncle Martin backed the cart into the shed to unharness the horse as the rain began to drum down around him. The downpour continued as we sat down to boiled eggs, homemade bread and newly churned butter. My, how we had missed the taste of fresh eggs and butter. In Dublin we were reduced to wartime dried eggs, margarine and grey bread that didn't encourage going back for a second slice. We hated the taste of margarine so much that my mother resorted to taking a tip from Granny Redmond and fried our bread in pork fat to make it edible. I was glad we were not a household who bothered with Grace- before- meals, because thanking God for his bounty would have seemed hypocritical. This did not prevent the Ma lamenting the fate of all the starving children in the world, and our base ingratitude for moaning about the quality of the food put before us.

The rain brought the whole Qualter family home, apart from Maureen who was working in the American Bar in Eyre Square.

'Well nobody will need a bath tonight' said a dripping Lackie as he propped his bicycle up against the gable end of the house.

'Stay out there the lot of ye' shouted Bid, barring entry to the house.

'Get them dry clothes' she told Winnie

'Ye lot, take yourselves off to the barn and strip off, I won't have ye dripping water all over my house' said Bid.

'Isn't it great that it's *her* house today, but it will be *our* house tomorrow when something needs mending, grumbled Tom to his father?

'Howld your whisht or ye'll get no tay' said Bid.

Perhaps it's time to explain the meal system in Claregalway at the time;

Breakfast - self explanatory

Lunch - didn't exist

Dinner - main meal of the day; Eaten around mid day

Snack - no such thing

'A bite to eat' or 'something in your hand' offered to visitors or children between meals.

Tea, on the go all day as opposed to 'Tea'- the meal

Tea - meal eaten on return from school or work

Supper - sandwich or leftover's any time before bedtime

It was always wonderful to see Lackie. He was a lovely man and at twenty eight showed no sign of thinking about getting married. Tom at thirty, the quietest, tallest and handsomest brother also seemed content to live at home, while Johnny, raising twenty and working as Bina's General Factotum, attended every dance and social event in the locality in an effort to meet a willing woman. The Qualter men didn't do as well in the hair stakes as the Qualter women, having the beginnings of widow's peaks by their late twenties. Despite having very few material possessions they were a happy family, full of goodwill, and praised as good neighbours. Living in Gortcloonmore down a bog road you'd think they'd be short of visitors, but not a bit of it, unless the road was impassable, there was always an extra place needed at the table. But this evening was different. The rain had eased off during tea, and we had just said the Angelus when the sky clouded over again. 'Well, nobody will be darkening our doorstep tonight' said Winnie. 'It might clear up yet' responded an ever hopeful Johnny, 'Kerins said he'd come over to welcome ye' he said, looking at Bridie and me.

'We're in for a storm' said Uncle Martin looking out at a darkening angry sky.

'Somebody's been annoying God today'.

I was well used to local weather descriptions which were usually very apt.

'Ye could drown ducks today' meant lashing rain.

'Tis cold enough to freeze souls' indicated a bitterly cold day.

'T'would take the breath outha ye and the goodness outha mushrooms' described frost.

'Tis mouldy weather for leather' characterized damp and dismal and

'Tis a quare day altogether' denoted mild but uncertain.

'A good day for the slaning' was a fine and dry day while

'The wind would rip the eyes outha your head' meant seriously windy, but

'Tis a safety pin day' labelled it breezy enough to lift a girls dress on a bike.

'Tis a fine soft day was common to mizzle or drizzle, less typical was the 'God be with the work' fine warm harvesting weather, or a week or so of 'Dog days' which were humid and still.

'Best get the stock in' Uncle Martin said, rising and putting his cap back on. We were playing pontoon when we heard the first rumble of thunder in the distance. 'That's over Annaghdown way' he said counting the seconds before the first flash of lightening. Annaghdown was in the next Parish about five miles away and was where the Loftus family originated. According to Martin they were 'Spalpeens' from Lisheenanoran, originally from Co. Mayo who used to come over to Claregalway for employment to earn 2/6d a day during the potato lifting 'and to steal our turf on the way home' Lackie would add.

The door was still open so we went outside to watch. It was safe enough to enjoy the spectacular display of jagged bolts of lightning arching from sky to ground, and from cloud to cloud, and to watch while red, orange and yellow balls thrown as if by an unknown hand whizzed across the sky, and blue jets of light shooting upwards through the top of the clouds. I had never seen a firework display, but imagined it must be like this. We were all so mesmerized that it took a crack of thunder practically overhead to make us realize the storm was heading our way.

'Jesus, Mary and Holy St Joseph' shouted Winnie as she shook with fright. 'We'll all be kilt' was her dire prediction.

Uncle Martin, ever the practical one had his sons marshalled and ready to follow commands, Tom to stay with the horse, Lackie with the cows. Johnny to man the stirrup pump in case anything caught fire and he would stay with the calves. Bid, in the middle of a Rosary when we piled into the house, was already seeing to it that Jesus, Mary and the Holy St Joseph knew about our blight. The storm was now overhead, the rain lashing down, huge cracks of thunder and the lightning bolts reflected on the walls of the room. Winnie, Bridie and I knelt down to join Bid. We were barely through our first 'Se do bheatha, a Mhuire' before there was another heartfelt

'*Oh, Jesus, Mary and Holy St Joseph*' from Winnie.

'Mammy', she said to Bid 'There's no lightening conductor on the house, 'remember it came down in the February gale, and Dada hasn't put it back up'.

My knowledge of Irish curses and recriminations was still sparse but I recognized 'amadan **mor**'. Bid got up off her knees and went to get her supply of Knock Water and liberally sprinkled us, and the house, as God now appeared to be aiming lightning bolts directly at our thatched roof. I hoped that He, Jesus, Mary, and the Holy St Joseph were sitting within communication distance of each other watching over our dilemma. We were unscathed, but not everybody escaped misfortune, several local cows and sheep were struck, and a couple of barns caught fire, but God was thanked when nobody lost their lives, however the stories of 'near misses' proliferated throughout our holiday.

Chapter 31; Loughgeorge

The following morning was sunny and warm drying the dew on the grass by the time we sat down to breakfast. We heard the rattle of a cart approaching the yard, and going to the door saw Kerins alighting.

'Well how are the girleens' he said smiling at Bridie and me?

We were pleased to see him and delighted to hear that he had come to take us out to Sarah's new home in Loughgeorge. Loughgeorge was little more than a road junction that straddled the parishes of Claregalway and Lackagh. The junction comprised of a few houses, the Garda Síochána Station and Roddy Kelly's pub. It also gave one the opportunity of taking the road to Tuam and onwards to Mayo, or curving right and heading for Roscommon and eventually Dublin. From Bid's we took the road back to Cloonbiggen and went straight along through Gortadooey, the road to Waterdale on our left, before we came to Sarah's rented little thatched cottage on the corner of the Loughgeorge road junction. Being set on the side of the road it had a lot in common with Mary Casserly's, but was twice the size, and had a back door , and small cottage garden to the side with a well structured clamp of turf, undercover, out the back. The house looked very familiar until I realized that it was Seanmháthair furniture that made it seem so. The most spectacular thing about Sarah's new home was the pink damask roses climbing up the walls. The smell was intoxicating and memorable, and completely outshone any need for Evening in Paris. She had few neighbours apart from the Kelly's in the Pub and the Garda Station; I only remember the Kyne's and Gillespie's. Sarah's baby, Margaret, was a sweet natured baby and very tolerant of being carried around, and bounced up and down, by her Dublin cousins. The Ma had sent a parcel of clothes that Bridie and I had outgrown, which delighted Sarah. They had been sent pre war from Julia, my mother's Aunt, and Martin's sister in Indianapolis, so were of good quality.

We talked about Seanmháthair and life in Cloonbiggen and I realized that I had a very sketchy view of the farming year. Being summer children we never saw the hard work that went into preparing the land, the ploughing, spreading dung, then harrowing, and drilling in the seeds for wheat, oats and barley crops. Mangles, turnips and potatoes had to be planted, thinned, harvested and saved in trenches over winter. Beet likewise, but being a cash crop it was sold, not saved. We had often seen the corn being cut and stuked but had always missed the threshing, and bringing home the ricks of turf from the bog; We never saw the calves and lambs being born early in the year, but had been around when Aunt Mays baby turkeys had hatched at the end of summer, and learned that rearing turkeys was difficult. They had remarkably casual and careless mother's, and were incredibly stupid hatchlings that couldn't get off their backs when they toppled over, but, despite their stupidity, most of them lived to fulfill their destiny on the Christmas table. Sarah was raising six such hatchlings having put some of Aunt May's eggs under a clucky hen. The poor hen was distracted and puzzled to have produced such moronic offspring. Sarah had very little space for livestock but with the fields of home nearby she was fattening some young bullocks. She needed a cow but had nowhere to house it. Mick was in some negotiations with Roddy Kelly to rent a field across the road. In the meantime Kerins was providing them with milk. Mick came home early afternoon having finished his round, and after his dinner walked us back as far as Cloonbiggen.

Kerins had told us he would be turning hay at the Holland's farm so Mick dropped us there as he went further on to his strip of bog to turn his turf. Delia was delighted to see us and gave us some cool buttermilk. Her three boys John, Michael and Bobby were out in the fields helping the men turn the hay. Kathleen and May were both on top of half made ricks built before the storm, pulling the top sodden layer off and tamping the ricks back into shape.

Bridie and I spent the rest of the afternoon playing in the fields until Kerins was ready to take us back to Bid. While harvesting hay was hard work it was also one of the great social events of the year when neighbours sons and daughters got to know each other, and parents had the opportunity of speculating on future matches and dowries.

Chapter 32; God Willing

Martin Qualter, born 1874, was seventy one and still an active man, but now, due to rheumatism in his hands and lower arms, the tasks he could do were restricted. However this didn't stop him causing himself unnecessary pain, and Bid endless exasperation, when he tried to do things he could no longer manage. Every evening the house reeked of Camphorated Oil as Bid applied it to his hands and arms before he went to bed, and every morning she dosed him with Cod Liver Oil. He had more or less given over the management of the place to Lackie and Winnie, with Tom and Johnny helping out at weekends but he still made the decisions, kept hold of the purse strings, and remained master of the house.

He was seventh of nine children of a mother widowed at forty four. They were Catherine, John, Thomas, Mary (my grandmother), William and Julia. Two previous William's died in childhood. The third William never married, and must have died before this point in time, because I have no recollection of him at all. Martin was a laconic man who seldom smiled but who had a wry sense of humour. He led an orderly life, and tried to align his farming year to the whims of Mother Nature. His weather forecasting skills were well regarded, so at hay cutting time and corn harvesting his neighbours sought his advice. This was freely given but always contained the rider '*God Willing*' to absolve him from blame if the weather didn't hold. Despite farmers and fishermen's dependence on information about the weather, forecasting was censured during the Emergency for fear of breaking neutrality agreements and aiding the Lufthansa.

Martin's greatest treasure was a cardboard box full of letters and photographs of Tom and Julia's families in Indiana. The letters were falling apart from unfolding and folding. Although bilingual he could barely read or write but he knew the contents of the letters by heart. It had been nearly four years since a postman had brought a letter with an American stamp out to Gortcloonmore, so to have two on the same day was an event long remembered by the family, and the neighbours.

Reading the accumulated news took some time, so Winnie and Lackie were kept busy, as neighbours came over at all hours to hear the letters read. However once Uncle Martin was able to handle the gist of the contents he went back to Montiagh, then off to Cloonbiggen, Loughgeorge, Waterdale and Bina's to spread the news from Indiana. Lackie covered the Feeney's, Kaney's and Noone's all related by intermarrying returning with messages and news to be sent on to the exiles. Although there was no letter from Bid's brother John there was news of him and his family in Tom's letter. Responding to the letters was a mammoth job, and to be undertaken by Winnie. Notepaper, envelopes, blotting paper and a new nib for the pen had to be bought from Hughes' post office. Ink was borrowed from Bid Greally, the nib attached to the old school pen, and Sunday afternoon set aside for the task in hand.

Winnie sat by the small table under the window to get the light.
She had an old yellowing school copy book in front of her and a pencil in her hand. In the copy book were drafts of letters written years before, because Uncle Martin liked to remember what news had already been recounted, and it saved the foolish waste of good notepaper if the writer made mistakes. The letter to Tom's family was drafted first. When Winnie suggested that she copy the same letter to Julia in Indianapolis, the look that Uncle Martin flashed her was enough to root her to the spot. Julia would have news of her own, the same news as Tom's family, just coached in different terms. John Noone would also have his own letter. Fingers covered in ink, blotting paper well used, two hours later the letters were ready for posting. Winnie, her tongue at the ready to lick the envelopes, was stayed by her father 'Don't seal them yet', he ordered. 'We might think of something to add later'. It was said by many that Winnie Qualter had the patience of a saint, but anybody witnessing her kicking the pig bucket around the yard following this injunction might have thought otherwise.
The Qualter's loved nothing more than having neighbours around to pass the time on winter evenings. Although the gatherings were small and the pleasures simple people walked or cycled in dire conditions to attend them, and their settle bed saw more use than most. Mick Madden's arrival was always heralded by the sound of his bicycle bell. He had a fine

voice and an encyclopedic knowledge of songs so was welcomed by more than Sarah. One of the Duggan neighbours could play the fiddle, Willie Forde the accordion, Uncle Mat the penny whistle and Tom the bodhrán. There was more than one Senachaí. The one I remember was Mike Silke who had a store of accounts of Turloughmore Fairs and local folklore about the *Bean Sí* and *Pisreoga* which were mostly lost to me because he relayed them in Gaelic but his begobs, begorrahs and 'by me sawel (soul)' 'my troth on it' and 'faith would have it' was the only cursing that was done and needed no translation. Brid Duggan was a *sean-nós singer*, who kept time with her foot as she sang taking us from the grief of 'Tá na Páipéir na Saighneál' to the fun of 'Caoirigh na Japs' but always in the background was the metronome beat of the old pendulum clock. In summer time people worked long days, so gatherings were fewer but we still became proficient at singing Uncle Martin's favourite Percy French songs. We knew every word to Phil the Fluter's Ball, Come back Paddy Reilly, Mountain's of Mourne, Abdul Abulbur Amir, and in years to come, Lackie, to shorten the road, would have us march along the bog road to Slattery's Mounted Foot, or the old 18th century quick march, Oro 'se do Bheatha Abaile. But the best fun of all was lilting as Winnie and the Holland girls, who 'handled their feet well' glowed with the effort of dancing the 'Queen of the Rushes' jig or 'The Blackbird' reel as Tom increased the beat of the bodhrán, or screaming with laughter at Lackie and Johnny doing the brush dance accompanied by Willie Forde, fingers racing up and down the accordion. In years to come Gael Linn used the Qualter house to record music and folklore stories which are now in some long forgotten archive.

The Qualters was known as a dry house but that is not to say that the men did not sthep outside when the desire to whet their whistle overcame them.

The rest of 1945, passed without anything memorable happening, and without finding out why the Ma had been called from the pulpit, everyone I asked was very vague about it. Too vague

It was the following year I killed the Canon.

Chapter 33; The Day the Canon Roared

1946 saw Bridie, and I back in Claregalway again for the summer.

I was now considered old enough to avoid the Sidhe-gaoithe and walk between Gortcloonmore and Cloonbiggen, and even on to Loughgeorge, but not out on the main road up to Cregboy. We were also of an age when we enjoyed playing with other children so instead of spending most of our time with the Qualter's we would this year stay with Aunt May for several weeks.

With the freedom of the farm and the fields we had endless fun. We also had our 'jobs' to do, collecting eggs, feeding calves, mucking out, sweeping the yard and a hundred and one other chores that Aunt May would think of, if you were rash enough to get under her feet, or sin of sins, indicate you were bored.

It was a dry summer so one of our daily tasks was to go down to the well near the river and bring home buckets of water. Although Winnie Duggan was only four she had had a great growth spurt, and was now nearly the same height as me at seven and a half, so we were well matched for water carrying. After several trips we had it down to a fine art. We had tied some old rags around the handle of the pail and had calculated how much water we could carry without it slopping over

On one of our trips we noticed Canon Moran hitting balls down Hession's field. At this distance in time I can't remember whether it was a golf putter or a hurling stick he was using but the balls were being whacked way down the field. Legend has it that it was golf balls though he was a mighty hurler in his time. Canon Moran, the local Parish Priest for thirty years, was a ferocious man, feared and disliked by many of his parishioners and an object of terror to my mother, whom he had called from the pulpit. Seeing him I remembered I still hadn't found out why. He was a well known Gaelic scholar and advocate of speaking Irish, but children who attended the local school had nightmares about being singled out for his attention during his frequent visits, the school being next to the Parish house where he lived, with his niece Molly keeping house for him. On our way back with the water the Canon in mid swivel cast his hawk like eye on Winnie and me. He imperiously beckoned us over and in machine gun Irish indicated that he wanted us to run down the field and gather in the balls. I was normally a compliant child, but when bullied there lay within me a streak of stubbornness that had been put to the test in the past, and now the Canon was going to tamper with it. I was nearly catatonic with fear at what I was going to do, and was fairly certain that either God, or, more likely, the Canon, was going to strike me dead. 'I'm sorry Father, said I, finding my voice, 'but we've got to get home with this water'. Winnie, who was preparing to sprint down the field, looked at me in horror, and at the Canon like a startled hare in a beam of light. He repeated this order several times, with him becoming more and more apoplectic with rage at each refusal on my part. At some point I realized that I had reached a plateau beyond terror and prepared for death.

Eventually he roared at me 'Who are your people?'

Before I could answer him I saw Don Quixote sitting bareback on a horse by the wall of Hession's field, observing the confrontation. Pat Cullinan, son of Molly, at twenty two was not as tall as the Canon, who was a good six foot, but I felt sure he could take the Canon on if hand to hand combat was called for, and would do even better if weapons were chosen since he was carrying a pitchfork.

'Clear off home' he advised us, 'I'll deal with this'

Winnie and I were quite sure Aunt May would hear the story, but as the days passed and with a new baby to keep her busy, nothing was said apart from the quiet teasing of Pat 'Ah, if it isn't the girl who made the Canon roar' he'd whisper every time he saw me. Then one morning Mary Casserly came running in with the astonishing news that Canon Moran was dead. 'The Canon's dead' 'the Canon's dead' the Canon's dead' she repeated like a demented parrot, dancing with glee.

'May he rest in peace' said Aunt May tearfully as she went on making bread. I looked across at Bridgie who had tears in her eyes too.

But once we got out in the barn Bridgie joined in our euphoria, and it soon became plain that the only one to mourn the Canon was Marteen who had been one of his altar boys. The funeral was a grand affair and was attended by Eamonn DeValera, the Taoiseach at the time. When I mentioned the latter to Granda Redmond his, not unexpected, but disgusted response was 'did nobody think to bring a gun with them'?

During the haymaking the following week Bridgie and I were bringing tea up to Uncle Mick and the helpers. Pat Cullinan and Mattie Carr were lolling against a newly tied rick when Pat winked at me and said 'Ah, the girl who killed the Canon'

'What do you mean' said Mattie Carr my best friend Mary's brother. 'Well, that's our secret' said the traitor, who went on teasing me about killing the Canon for years. However, to give him his due I don't think he told anybody apart from Mattie who was also terrible tease. It was years before it dawned on me that it was more likely to have been *him* tackling the Canon that has killed him. Bridgie quizzed me on the way home but I knew I could never tell her, and Winnie would never tell *anybody* because if Aunt May ever found out our lives wouldn't be worth living, me for disobeying the Canon, and Winnie for joining me. It would be useless claiming blind terror was responsible for the latter, not free will.

When Bridie and I returned to Dublin we found that Sean had spent most of the summer with Granny Redmond. It was also noticeable that Gran was coming on a daily basis to cook, and that she and the Ma were getting on a lot better, although there was still some teeth sucking on the Grans part, and raising of eyebrows or eyes cast to heaven on the Ma's. My father as usual was busy with his Union activities but made an effort to be at home at weekends. This resulted in fewer rows, and made my mother easier to live with. I hadn't managed to annoy her for so long that I decided to try my hand at it one day, to have Gran say 'Leave your Mother in peace, she's not well'. This was a revelation since we had not seen a doctor crossing the doorstep, there was no evidence of any medicine around the place, and biggest surprise of all, Gran was defending her. Being a self centered eight year old I don't remember being unduly worried. Life went on as before except we now had a washer woman who took our laundry, and returned it washed and ironed every week and Mary Kelly, daughter of John and Ellen Kelly from Waterdale, Delia's help, and related by blood ties to both our families, came frequently from Dundrum with offerings of poultry and other treats. Delia herself was then terminally ill so her thoughtfulness was beyond measure.

The New Year of 1947 and the month leading up to it was the coldest winter in decades. To try to keep some heat in, our eight pane Regency windows were kept shuttered, leaving a one foot gap at the top for daylight. Coal was still rationed as were other commodities and we seemed to live in constant gloom. The muffles clip clop of Mr. Gaffney's horse drawn coal cart became a rare sound as it went around the icy streets with sacks on its feet and we became used to managing with turf. Being an expert on turf I knew that this turf had not been turned enough to season so we had to pile it on either side of the fireplace to dry it enough to use it without choking on the smoke. The Ma had to choose a turf imbued household or freeze to death, so Paddy Duffy, a boy of my age who lived nearby, and whom I knew from his round collecting food scraps to feed his mothers pigs began collecting our turf from the turf depot near the 27 Steps in Summerhill. Aran jumpers, which we had scorned in the past, now became our daily wear, and Gran wrapped brown paper around our torso's underneath our liberty bodices. I refused to have my chest rubbed with goose fat, but from the smell of some of my fellow scholars their Grannies' had obviously been more successful than mine.

Seán had started school the previous September, and loved it. He settled in with a head start because he could already read. Education was segregated back then, so although our school was under the same roof it had separate boys and girls entrances, and playgrounds. All we heard from him was Mrs. Kavanagh this, and Mrs. Kavanagh that, so he obviously liked his teacher, Mrs. Kavanagh. He still had his curls which should have been an obvious source of teasing; instead he was called GikGik by his new friends, the nickname being chosen because of the large brown mole on the calf of one of his legs. Some wag made up a song, to the air of the Blue Danube, which we used to torment him with as we whirled around singing;

'It's all on your leg GikGik la, la,

It's five inches thick, GikGIK la, la.

It's nice to taste GikGik la, la.'

I don't remember any more, which is probably just as well.

The bone stabbing cold came back the end of February and continued well into the month of March, but the thaw did not come until April. The snow and wind was quite severe on the last Friday in February when a 24 hr blizzard set in. Driven by a fierce east wind straight from Siberia it paralysed Dublin. We huddled around the radio listening to news of similar conditions which were being reported from all over the country where huge snow-drifts, some up to fifteen feet high were experienced.

We kept being sent home from school because of the inefficiency of the school boiler. There are only so many snowball fights you can have, or killer ice slides you can make, before getting bored or freezing to death. We all had terrible chilblains and Ma spent most of her days in bed, or wrapped up in an eiderdown in an armchair playing the gramaphone. My parents bed had been moved into the front room where the fire was kept going. There were days when Gran and Granda could not get out of their flat. They lived nearby in Upper Buckingham Street which was on a hill, and the local kids had turned both the pavements and parts of the road into some of the most spectacular slides in Dublin. To ensure the continuation of the fun, buckets of water were surreptitiously sluiced down the slides before bedtime and Jack Frost left to do the rest.

Sometime in January the postman delivered a notification saying that there was a crate and two parcels to be picked up at the Summerhill Depot. The Da came back from the Depot, with a laden pram that had serviced his children for years, but which he was pushing for the first time in his life. There was a big label that said 'Perishable' on the crate, and all three items were covered in American stamps and customs forms. As the Da wrestled with the crate, Gran started on one of the parcels. It needs stating here and now that Gran was a hoarder of string, brown paper, buttons, safety pins, hat pins and sundry other items, so the crate was long opened before the string on the parcel was undone. The smell that rose from the crate was strange and exotic. The customs form had declared 'Oranges' but I had no idea what an 'Orange' was. Ma pulled back the fine straw packing, and there they were about twelve dozen oranges wrapped individually in tissue paper illustrated with the picture of an Orangery all the way from the Loftus family in Sonoma California. I'd like to say we were fed up eating them, but in fact we saw very few of them. As news of their arrival spread far and wide so did their distribution. The other parcels contained clothes from Julia Qualter in Indiana which pleased Ma no end. I was not so grateful. The main item of clothing I got was a brown and yellow herringbone tweed coat which had room for me to 'grow into'. Having 'grown into' it I was not allowed to 'grow out' of it without having two inch brown velour strips added to the cuffs and hem. God, how I hated that coat! It was then inherited by Bridie and finally Maureen Duggan. When it reached Maureen, Aunt May took it apart and turned it inside out giving it a new lease of life as a yellow and brown herringbone coat. As Martin Feeney would say 'There was a fine bit of cloth in it'.

Chapter 35; Intimations of Mortality

Shortly after Bridie's sixth birthday in February, when we were once again off school, the Ma told us she was going to die. Well it wasn't quite as stark as that. Shortly after dinner she had got back into bed with her jewellery box, a box we were forbidden to touch without her permission, and then under supervision. I watched her dividing the contents into three, take three lace trimmed white cotton hankies and put the selected contents on the hankies. She told us to sit on the bed, and matter-of-factly said to Gran, 'I think it's time to tell them.'

'The Doctor say's I have a weak heart, and I'm going to die' Ma announced. 'When', somebody said, probably me. 'Maybe in a few months' Ma replied 'I'm telling you because I might have to go into hospital and I don't want you to worry.'

She then went on to explain that we would live with Gran and Granda because Da wanted us to stay in Dublin. Gran nodded in agreement saying 'Of course you can still go to Galway for your holidays'.

This proposal sounded ok so far, but would need consideration and careful balancing of the pros and cons.

'I'm dividing these few things among you' Ma said, 'Granny will keep them for you until you are grown up'.

 I would like to be able to write about how heartbroken we had been by this news, and to report that we threw our arms around Ma, and hung on her neck sobbing, but it would be a fabrication. What we actually did was to start squabbling about our inheritance. I wanted the beaded turquoise necklace being left to Bridie, who wanted the green and gold lustre powder compact which was one of my items, and Seán wanted the cigarette lighter *right no*w. I would also like to believe our indifference was because her impending death appeared unreal. Life went on as usual apart from the three of us spending weekends with Granda and Gran. Granda was a retired Lighterhouse man who has worked on the Liffey for about thirty years. He was a designated fireman on the tug and had worked until he was well into his sixties. Born in Stradbally Co. Laois he has some sympathy for my mother as a fellow *culchie* but had no time for her airs and graces. I have no memory of anybody coming up from Claregalway apart from Roddy Kelly who came frequently. Perhaps her impending death at thirty nine was as unreal to them as it was to us. There was a lot more involvement in our life now from Sheila, my father's sister. Sheila had two very young children but she and Christy took us out in their car on Sundays, weather permitting.

On Sunday 20th April that Sheila told us that Ma had died during the night. Gran had left to go and wash her, and lay her out, with the help of Mrs. Mc Auley our downstairs neighbour, so Granda was dishing up the dinner, a remarkable occurrence in its own right. Sheila took us back home to say 'Good bye'. Like Seanmháthair, the same rituals had been observed except that my mother had a blue Legion of Mary shroud, and somebody had crimped and dressed her hair the way she liked it. I t was the thoughtfulness of this last gesture that brought tears to my eyes but I didn't cry. We said our 'Goodbyes' and left the family to Wake her so the next time I saw her was when she was lowered into the ground in Glasnevin. However my preoccupation at that point in time was looking for a lost five year old brother. 'Hold his hand, and don't lose him,' Gran had said as we stepped out of Jennings funeral car, but within minutes the little bugger had disappeared behind rows of gravestones. Not to draw attention to the fact, or to desecrate a graveyard by shouting, I set out to find him accompanied by one of Jennings drivers. A mourner putting flowers on a grave saw us, and as we approached pointed to a small boy about twenty graves to my left.

'There are an awful lot'a dead people in here, said he, calmly surveying the rows of graves.

'Yes, and there'll be one more if you let go of my hand again.' said I.

The liveried driver treated him with a bit more kindness by luring him back to the graveside with a gob full of aniseed balls.

My mother died from mitral stenosis, a result of childhood rheumatic fever. Four pregnancies in four years had no doubt weakened her heart. Julia her second child had died within twenty four hours of birth.

Two weeks later I made my First Communion dressed like a miniature bride as a result of Ma's judicious saving of clothing coupons and the Grans shopping expertise. Following Mass the First Communicants were taken back to the drill hall in the convent to have breakfast, and having fasted from bedtime, to break our fast. It was Sr. Francis, my class teacher, who was to prove my undoing. 'Well, aren't you a credit to your Granny, and to your poor Mother looking down on you from heaven', she enthused.

I must have cried for an hour.

Chapter 36; The Eye of the Storm

Having made my first communion I was now expected to be forever in a state of grace, and to avoid the occasion of sin. I still wasn't very well versed on sins, so examining my conscience before going to confession became a weekly worry. What with God, Jesus, the Blessed Virgin and all the Saints looking down on me, Seanmháthair and my Mother watching over me, and my Guardian Angel by my side, not many occasions for committing sins arose. I still didn't understand four of the Ten Commandments, at least one of the seven deadly sins, and when it came to sins of commission or omission Sr. Francis lost me for a while. I knew the difference between heaven, hell, and purgatory but it was Tommy Duggan who introduced me to Limbo

The summer of 1947 we were back in Claregalway, this time staying mainly at Aunt May's but occasionally being kidnapped by the Qualter's for overnight stays. Seán spent most of his time with them in Gortcloonmore because he loved all the attention he got from Bid Noone and Winnie. Aunt May was busy with Johnny born the previous year so he was quite happy to be an only child, rather than the one of many under Aunt May's roof. When we saw him near the end of the holidays he had a mop full of curls which Winnie used to delight in putting into rag curlers at night, doing so without any protest from him. He looked like Shirley Temple.

The best day of the week was Monday. Monday was Aunt Mays wash day. **Obair ó chrích obair bean tí and** Monday was Aunt May's marathon day. Aunt May fretted all day if Monday was wet. To have to put off doing the washing threw her whole week out of kilter. As far as Aunt May was concerned we ceased to exist on Mondays, which was fine by us, because Mondays were freedom days. Once we did our 'jobs' we were free as birds to wander where we liked, Aunt May's injunctions not to go near the river, not to annoy the neighbours, not to eat or drink anything from Bina Lenihan's kitchen, and not to go cross the field with the bull in it, were all ignored. Tommy and I decided the bull in the field was unavoidable unless we wanted to do a big detour to Lydican Lisheen. We had been there several times without mishap and today was a special day because Tommy was going to say Mass. To prepare the alter we needed flower vases. I had seen Aunt May scalding empty jam jars so suggested we take some to meet our purpose. Tommy, like me, had made his First Communion in May, and like me was very interested in sin. Tommy had discovered a great injustice. When he had been over in Lydican hazel grove, picking nuts for Christmas, he had learned about the Lisheen and had been outraged.

'Babies who are born dead, or who die before they are baptised are buried here' he told me, the first time he took me there.

'They're not allowed in the graveyard because it's consecrated ground' he explained, neither of us having a clue what consecrated ground was, but construing an injustice.

It was actually quite difficult to decide whether a stone marker was a grave or not, because there were no headstones or crosses. A peaceful meadow setting with just cows and sheep grazing was a lovely place for dead babies but we felt that these babies had been blamed for something that was not their fault and should be buried with their dead mammy's and daddy's.

'They're living in Limbo', Tommy told me, which he explained was like living in a fog, where you couldn't see anybody.

Tommy then decided that if the priest wouldn't say Mass for them, he would. There was only one problem with this, Mass in 1947 was said in Latin and neither of us knew much, however Tommy was in training as an altar boy and had heard Marteen rehearsing his alter server's responses often enough to be able to repeat them, so we would have a very modified service. My part was to fill the jars with meadow flowers, to ring a bell created from a stone in a jam jar at crucial moments and to say the occasional, 'Sanctus' and 'Amen'.

When we returned home we were feeling very virtuous, and apart from walking through the *pairc na tairbh* twice, we had every reason to be.

We heard Aunt May before we saw her. She was incandescent with rage, as she drubbed one of Uncle Mick's shirts with the crusheen, a long handled wooden paddle used for washing the mud off potatoes and for pounding clothes. Sunlight suds flew everywhere. Although she was doing a lot of shouting there wasn't a soul in sight, her only audience being three bewildered ducks.

The old nursery rhyme went across my brain

'Wash on Monday

Iron on Tuesday

Bake on Wednesday

Scrub on Thursday

Churn on Friday

Shrive on Saturday

Mass on Sunday'

'Come here ye little shuliers' she ordered us.

'What have ye been up to' she demanded to know,

'Nothing Mammy' said Tommy, which I thought was a mistake.

'What do ye mean *nothing'* shouted an enraged Aunt May

'God grant me patience' *What* have ye been up to' she repeated.

'We've being praying', I told her.

That stopped her in her tracks.

'Praying', she said with some incredulity?

Words flashed through my brain -bull - Lisheen - praying - trouble, but graves - praying - graveyard - acceptable.

'We went to the graveyard to pray for dead people' said I, trying to look virtuous and endeavouring not to tell an out and out lie.

'Did ye go near the river' she wanted to know,

'Of course not Mammy' said an equally virtuous looking Tommy.

'Did ye annoy Bina Lenihan', now *that* was a double barrelled question *meaning* 'Did you go to see Bina *and* eat anything from her kitchen?'

'No Mammy' said a now indignant Tommy.

We were about to slink off, when she asked the killer question,

'Have either of ye seen my jam jars'

'No.' Instant - duplicate - survival - duplicitous - denial.

The thief who took her priceless jam jars that she had scalded ready for reuse had more curses heaped his head than the monster that murdered Nell Flaherty's drake. Fortunately for us, Aunt May believed that it had been an innocent journeyman who had mended a bucket for her.

We could have gone back to the Lisheen and retrieved the jars, but we didn't even contemplate it, feeling it would be a betrayal of our dead babies. I also had a feeling that Aunt May would resurrect her investigation if they just reappeared, and that Tommy would crack. He lacked my experience under my late Ma's inquisitional despotic regime. On Saturday I didn't have much difficulty preparing for confession, and I now knew the difference between a sin of commission and a sin of omission

Aunt May was a woman of many talents. Like farmers wives all over the country she worked from dawn to well past dusk rearing children, chickens, ducks, geese and turkeys, milking cows, feeding and mucking out pigs, bucket feeding calves, churning butter, making, mending, washing and ironing clothes, cooking for an ever ravenous family, helping out neighbours and attending to her religious duties. She was blessed with an understanding and patient husband in Mick Duggan, a descendent of one of the five branches of the Montiagh Duggan's recorded in the Tithe Aplotments Book of 1827 as paying the tithe on 300 acres in Montiagh "in commonage". Uncle Mick would take himself off to the barn, and ride out any storm brewing, however he was sensible enough to occupy himself with wife pleasing tasks while he was there, chopping logs, re-arranging a clamp of turf, tidying the straw loft, or mucking out.

Uncle Mick was a special man. He farmed during the transition period from horse to tractor, but never appeared happy with mechanisation. He loved the labours and joys of 'real' farming, ploughing, sewing, reaping and mowing, and spent his year answerable to God, the weather and seasons. He walked every foot of his land from Cuchullin's stone in the top field to the roadside haggard. He knew his land soft and firm, wet and drained, barren and fertile from fairy mounds* to mushroom patches. He had an eye for good stock but he was a rubbish barber sheering the hair of his four sons into a style ordained by the authorities as *de rigour* for juvenile criminals. Never happy in a collar and tie he only wore them to Mass and funerals. When Maureen was professed as a Sister of Mercy they had been removed long before the photographs were taken.

Aunt May's foibles were that she lacked a sense of humour, and set too much store by respectability, but compared to her sister, my deceased mother, she stood up well. Her storms were short lived, but you could feel the breeze from my Ma's for days.

For a decade to come Aunt May had Bridie, Sean and me, to stay for the long summer holidays and maintained a workload that few modern women could cope with. We all remember her with the greatest affection. Late in 1947 there was sad news for the Qualters. Tom died in Indiana age seventy, and with his passing, a link to the past for all of us.

Chapter 37; Thou Shalt Not

Why is it that a child invariably ignores an order when told not to do something? If Aunt May has told us to go and play by the river, annoy the neighbours, eat in Bina's kitchen, or go into the field with the bull, would we have taken any delight in circumventing her commands? I doubt it.

I don't know why Tommy and I set out to tease Mrs. Clancy who lived a field or two back the road. She has a fierce dog who barked incessantly when anybody approached the house, but for some reason this dog liked Tommy. He would come up with tail wagging and watch with interest as Tommy and I crept around placing eggs, stolen from Aunt May's hen house, in plain sight, but in the most unlikely places in Mrs. Clancy's garden, and he would then hide with us in the bushes. We would wait for Mrs. Clancy to appear at her scullery window when Tommy would do a fantastic imitation of a hen having laid an egg. He would do this several times until Mrs. Clancy was drawn out to look for the eggs of the out layers. Imagine her surprise when she found her eggs in a Y branch in a rose tree, on top of the gate post or nestling among some pink geraniums in a pot. We got away with this tease several times, and Mrs. Clancy's hens became renowned as the most eccentric hens that anyone had ever come across.

The Clare River that ran near Bina's and the 13th century Friary ruins were a big attraction being a glorious place to play. We used to lie on the memorial slabs pretending to be dead or looking up at the ever moving clouds talking or dreaming, or playing hide and seek ignoring the notices not to climb. To circumvent suspicion we could use the legitimate excuse that we were going to the graveyard to pray for our family dead, and to weed their graves and with only the rooks to spy on us we got away with murder. Dusk called us home because not only did we have the Bean Sí to worry about but blood sucking bats in the bell tower as well. Our bats were probably the common **pipistrelle** or the lesser horseshoe but Dracula had a lot to answer for back then.

The other big attraction in 1947 was that the Moore children had now come to live with Bina. Delia, their mother, my mother's friend and cousin, and my Godmother, had died the month before. They would no longer be just 'summer children' like us, but would live here all year round. Minnie Morris, a neighbour in Cregboy had long since christened us the Summer Children primarily because having 15 children of her own she could never remember our names. The Moore's were now old enough to come down on the train alone which filled me with envy. It would be another couple of years before we too would be put in charge of the Guard and be met off the train in Oranmore. John was about fourteen and rugby mad but girls were not on his agenda. He only played with Micheál and other boys so we saw little of him. Kathleen, a sophisticated thirteen was great fun, and more importantly had a stash of American Film Fan Magazines that she, Bridgie and I used to peruse. Kathleen's main preoccupation was acquiring a nose to equal Deanna Durbin's. This was difficult because although she had a well shaped nose the tip had a slight hook, so to correct this minor impediment, at every opportunity she had her index finger up under her nose tilting the tip up. Literally this made her one armed for most of the summer, curtailed many of our activities while we humoured her, and left a crease across her nose that would last for hours. Telling her she was committing one of the seven deadly sins was a waste of time. I have very little recollection of Marie the youngest Moore, age ten. She was just a lovely child with mischievous dimples who was happy to join in any adventure.

Going out the side gate of the Friary led to the river bank where we fished in the reeds for pinkeens, floated sticks and paper boats downstream or searched for animal bones from dead sheep. I loved watching the elegant gliding swans on the river, gazing on them wondering if any of them were descendents of the children of Lir. Fishing for 'pinkeens', or minnows, required jam jars containing a piece of bread that were sunk gently to the river bed, then pulled up again by two pieces of string around the neck to keep it steady, and not disturb any pinkeens that had gone inside to nibble the bread. The jars we borrowed from Bina who has never scalded a jam jar in her life, and who, if she made jam, would probably have emptied any surviving pinkeens out of them and poured in the jam.

Keeping our clothes dry was an overriding preoccupation. A visit to

Bina's kitchen we could get away with, if Maureen didn't tell tales. Being the only one of us with a conscience *and* suicidal tendencies, she didn't realize that confessing to Aunt May didn't automatically get you a free pardon. Aunt May's version of justice was one of joint enterprise, 'you participated and / or didn't stop what was going on, ergo you were an accomplice and guilty by association.' Her 'not guilty' verdicts were zero. Wet clothes were a dead giveaway. The girls therefore tucked their dresses into their knickers, and the Tommy rolled his short pants as high as they would go. There was a strict no splashing rule, however if the worst came to the worst we knew that Bina would dry our clothes in front of her hearth, because, despite Aunt May's dire warnings we never passed by without a visit to her kitchen. I still expected to see her mother, Kate, sitting by the hearth puffing on her little clay pipe, listening to the news.

By today's health and safety standards the Welfare Department would never allow Bina Lenihan to be the custodian of three pampered children from the middle class suburb of Dundrum. Bina's lack of hygiene was legendry. She always looked well scrubbed but never thought to change her wrap around apron, or clean anything. The snug was only swept when a regular would take a broom to the trekked in mud or manure that prevented him standing in a favourite spot. The bar was sticky from previous slops, but Bina was always generous if your glass stuck to the counter causing you any spillage. Glasses were dunked in a bucket of water to rinse them, but the bucket was often not emptied for days. However the mould covered tea towels probably produced enough Penicillin to counteract the bacteria in the water. The kitchen was nearly as bad. The floor was swept daily but the detritus instead of being swept out the door was brushed into the fire. The ancient fly paper hanging from the ceiling was full of skeletonised flies, and her cobwebs outshone Mrs. Haversham's in Great Expectations. The table was never scrubbed so always had evidence of bread making on it. We used to divert ourselves by seeing who could make the biggest ball of dough from the mixture of flour and cigarette ash we could rake in.

Bina would smile at us through her food flecked, and finger print encrusted, spectacles;

'Will ye have something in your hand before you go?' she would say coaxingly.

'Some 'rid' lemonade?' she would urge

'A few fig rolls? 'She would wheedle enticingly.

When it was just Tommy and me we never hesitated, but on days Bridgie was in loco parentis, and charged, on pain of death, by Aunt May, not to let food or drink past our lips in Bina's kitchen she could feel our beseeching eyes on her so would cave in, thanking Bina for her hospitality. A delighted Bina would take down her best glasses from the press, blow sharply into each one, set them out on the table, pour the red lemonade into them, and having carefully removing the dead flies and very much alive little spiders, pass the brimming glasses into our hands. Out of the same press would come a lovely porcelain cake plate with signs of previous use on it. With one eye closed from the smoke from the eternal cigarette in the corner of her mouth, a packet of fig rolls or custard creams would cascade onto the plate, inadvertently being sprinkled with ash as they did so. We left not a crumb or a dreg. It was great to be old enough to know better but too young to care. We knew that Bina's door was always open to us and her welcome assured. She was a great character who to this day is remembered by local families. The pub site has changed over the years becoming a riding stable and is currently used for farm storage. Being in a prime position on the main road it will no doubt fall to progress and will fade to memory, but for as long as it stands it remains a monument for those of us who knew and loved Bina dearly.

Granda Redmond died in April 1949 two weeks before Ireland became a Republic. Since Ireland had been a de facto republic since 1937 it would make very little difference to our lives. The biggest difference was that the King would no longer be signing letters on our behalf; we would have our own 'king' in the form of Douglas Hyde, the current President of Saorstat Éire. The only crumb of comfort that Granda extracted from the situation was that DeValera and Fianna Fail had been voted out of power the previous year, but it *was* only a crumb of comfort because he regarded most of our elected representatives as 'self serving hoors'. 'We live in a country ruled by gombeen men, gobshites and cute hoors' he would opine rattling his newspaper in irritation. Granda lived and died numbered among the proletariat. He would always have had more in common with Emiliano Zapata than Eamonn deValera. He died on his feet as he walked out of St Agatha's Church at the end of the ten o'clock Mass. From my classroom window across the street I heard the ambulance arrive, and we were informed by our teacher that a covered form had been put on a stretcher and driven away, but I had no idea it was Granda.

Seán was waiting at the Boy's gate for me to walk him home. He pointed at something hanging on the Church railings 'That looks like Granda's hat' he said, I went over and flicked the hat off the tall railings. An old, brown, fedora hat now lay on the ground. I picked it up and looked inside. It had the same type of leather sweat band as Granda's. I smelt it and it smelt of Granda. We ran all the way home but as soon as we came within sight of the Buildings we knew. Our blinds were drawn as were most of the neighbours.

We had been living with Gran and Granda for two years. Three young children had completely disrupted his life. At seventy three he should have been looking forward to a quiet retirement. He never once complained, but adjusted his daily routine to enjoy some peace by walking around the Quays, sitting under the poplar trees by the Royal Canal watching the horse led tugs bring turf from the bogs, or going into the Carnegie Free Library in Charleville Mall nearby, adjacent to my school, to read the daily papers and periodicals. He stood surety for my first Library Tickets which allowed me to borrow one non-fiction and two fiction books at a time from the Children's Library. I had long gone through every readable book in this section so when Granda died I took over his tickets for the Adult Library. The Librarian, who knew Granda, also knew he was dead but went through the charade of allowing me to take out books for him until I was old enough to apply for my own tickets, however once in a while he'd look at my choice and say

'I don't think John Redmond would be interested in that, put it back'.

Since the Irish Free State had some of the most stringent censorship laws in the Western world, God alone only knows what he was protecting me from.

Uncle Martin also died on his feet six months later. Bid found him in a crumpled heap replenishing hay in the cattle mangers. When we had been down for our holidays in the summer we had enjoyed several kidnaps from the Duggan's, spending occasional nights under his roof. Like Uncle Mick he was a traditional farmer, his one great regret was that none of his children showed any sign of getting married. Having enjoyed thirty four years with Bid he could not understand their reluctance, and threatened to 'cleamhnas' the lot of them.

He had every reason to be concerned because his genealogical branch finished with their deaths. Johnny died suddenly, aged forty, Tom, Lackie, Maureen and Winnie saw out their three score and ten. None of them married. Bid's health declined and she died in the Central Hospital in August 1954. Her one wish was to die at home but she was, by then, too ill to go back to Gortcloonmore.

They now all lie together in the family grave in Claregalway graveyard and their old derelict house still bears witness to the fact that they were last of their family line.

Chapter 39; The Fainne

'What is her name'?

'What is her date of birth?

'What does her father do?

Twelve years old, and Miss Divilly, teacher of Cailini at Scoil Bhaile Chlair na Gallimhe was treating me like a retarded five year old.

Bridgie was the one being questioned. Now I wouldn't have been so affronted if the questions were in Irish, and she was acting as my interpreter, but the questions were in English, and as a Dublin jackeen, English was my mother tongue. Since Ebhlin Divilly was under no obligation to register me I looked earnestly at her and kept my City gob shut.

Sr. Francis and Sr. Monica, Daughters of Charity, and teachers at my school in Dublin, had decided I was scholarship material. One of the requirements for passing the scholarship exam was that I needed to be able to pass a viva in Irish. You'd think that six years of DeValera's compulsory Irish in school, plus two months a year in a Gaeltacht area would have produced somebody functionally literate in the language. Well you'd be wrong. Unfortunately my Irish language education straddled the years of the great divide between the traditionalists and the modernizers, the old alphabet and the new alphabet, the old spelling and the new spelling, Connacht Irish versus An Caighdean Oifigiuil. Sr. Monica was fairly certain that the examiners would be old school, so it was decided that instead of going home at the end of the summer holidays I would be registered for the autumn term at Claregalway School and concentrate on 'old Irish'.

Miss Divilly's classroom was thirty five and a half feet by eighteen and a half feet, and was twenty feet high. It housed nearly forty girls with ages rising to fourteen years of age.

Like Molly Cullinan she was a wonderful organiser and juggled activities so that specific age groups got the best education she could provide. The 'big girls' helped out with the younger ones reading, and the little ones had play time outside when another group needed to concentrate. I don't remember an assistant teacher during my time there but apparently there was one employed. Compared to my convent school in Dublin the Claregalway curriculum was very basic, but the children probably had a better grasp of arithmetic than I did and they could all read. They were also well versed in Irish poetry and legends;

I learned about the deeds of *Finn Mac Cumhail*, and that *Cuchullin* had thrown a stone from the Devil's Causeway and it had landed in Mick Duggan's field. I knew the stony outcrop well. It hid the entrance to a fairy mound and round it grew the best mushrooms on the farm. We never picked them, leaving them for the 'Sidhe gaoithe' who often manifested themselves by a rush of hot wind as they passed by. It may only have been a *pisreoga* but as children we weren't taking any chances.

I also learned that fairy mounds are the homes (Shees) of the Sidhe gaoithe or 'Aos Sí'. In Irish lore many call them 'The Sidhe', but that is incorrect, sidhe being the Irish word for mound. Rather, they are Aos Sí, "People of the Mounds". 'The Sidhe' are a powerful supernatural race and are descendants of the pre-Celtic inhabitants of Ireland the "Tuatha Dé Danann" who settled in Ireland eons ago. When the Milesians invaded Ireland from Spain, they found these "people of the Goddess Danu" and fought and defeated them. As part of their surrender terms, the Tuatha Dé Danann agreed to retreat and dwell underground in the hollow hills, or sidhe, where it is said they remain to this day. They are often called the Kings and Queens of the Fairies; but they are neither winged nor pocket size like Tinkerbell. They are tall, with a noble appearance, sylvan of speech and are generally described as finely dressed and stunningly beautiful, though they can also be frightening ugly. They are sometimes described as transparent beings that walk without leaving tracts or making a sound, but when travelling they can sound like a swarm of bees. They are dressed very finely and their underground mounds are reported to be sumptuous.

Apart from a lack of books in the Duggan household except for a mildewed copy of Benjamin Cardozo's 'Law of Tort' and J.J. Roche's 'Life of John Boyle O'Reilly' with the first 32 pages missing I was enjoying school. Not least the fact that Miss Divilly didn't bother herself with homework, unlike the nuns who believed that a good hour an evening would keep you out of mischief, being big believers in an idle mind being the Devil's workshop. I was informed by a Dublin school friend that with the scholarship subjects this had now risen to two hours. At the end of a month Miss Divilly was disappointed to discover I was still speaking pidgin Irish though' she had to admit I could understand what she said. She interrogated me wanting to know how I could be making such little progress when everybody around me was speaking Irish to me. Indignantly I responded that *nobody* spoke Irish to me. While true, I was like the Priest in the Mulberry Bush, who, 'remembered too late on his thorny green bed, much that well may be thought cannot wisely be said.' Up to this point I was not aware that my classmates were supposed to speak in Irish in the playground, and 'when the opportunity arose', and that, likewise, the Duggan household would be expected to be a hotbed of Irish speakers. To encourage the use of the Irish language in the area De Valera gave £5 a year to all who spoke it, but since the School Inspector only checked once in a blue moon their reward was safe as long as I kept my mouth shut.

Everybody hated me.

Winnie Qualter's answer to the solution was for me to move in with them, but much as I loved them I didn't fancy a three mile walk to and from school every day. It was Lackie, who suggested the obvious, 'She needs a teacher, he said. And right across the road from Aunt May's was the answer to my problem, teacher, and mother of Don Quixote, Molly Cullinan.

Molly was a born teacher. For an hour a day after school I went across to her kitchen for Irish conversation, no writing, no spelling, just simple every day chat. Her own daughter Eileen was also having lessons, lessons to make her functionally literate in English. Eileen, in her late teens would much sooner have been out on farm with Pat. She was better than any farmhand, and could work like a Trojan. However you needed to give Eileen a wide berth when she was welding a pitchfork, being deaf she would not hear you coming so you would find yourself buried in hay, or worse, much worse. By the end of term Molly decided I had the right to wear a silver fainne, and gave me one she had earned herself. I passed the Irish viva. The Nuns had been right. The examiner has been born and raised in Connemara, and was very impressed with my Connacht accent and sentence structure. Thank God he didn't ask me to read or write.

With confirmation behind us and no Canon Moran to blight our teenage years we were allowed to go to the cinema in Galway on borrowed bikes, or to the pictures on our doorstep in Hanley's Hall. The films were always the same John Wayne or John Derek, Dracula or Frankenstein. We also now had music. The Duggan's had inherited my Ma's wind up gramaphone and records, so the big band sound was introduced to Claregalway. Unfortunately so were her records of Irish tenor, Joseph (bloody) Locke whom I detested.

Of course I'm factually inaccurate when I say 'teenagers'. There was no such thing as a teenager in the early nineteen fifties. We were young people, often young working people, because only the lucky few went on to secondary education. The noticeable difference between Dublin young people and Claregalway young people was that the latter kept to their own gender. Seating in the Church had always been segregated but even under the new regime of Fr. O'Dea it continued. The boys were either obsessed with the GAA, or joining the priesthood, while the girls were Legion of Mary devotees, attended meetings of the Total Abstinence Association, or joined a nunnery.

The biggest difference was that Tommy Duggan was no longer up for mischief. He became quiet and serious and a bit of a loner, not a great athlete, or holy enough to be a Priest he kept to the shadows and I remember little of him as a young man. However, whenever we had to pass the jam to each other at the table we would share a smile and remembered dead babies and bewildered ducks. Much to the disbelief of all, he died in his early forties.

   Apart from my cousins, Mary Carr was my only friend in Claregalway. We spent most of our time sitting on walls talking, or cycling around the countryside. Mary was an expert at keeping out of her mother's way. She had nothing to learn from me.

'For God's sake let's get out of here before she has us thinning turnips or pulling beet' she'd say on the run. She was also good at avoiding Mattie, eight years older, who every time he saw us would find some mucking out for us to do or something equally physical and disgusting.

Bridgie Duggan, on the other hand had become a full time farmers daughter. As the oldest girl she had taken a lot of work off her mother who had the added burden of a young child, Johnny, born in 1946. We still managed a lot of fun escaping to Sarah's house. She now had three more children Tommy, Fergus and Gerry and had moved to Killeen in Castlegar. We would raid her makeup box and splash ourselves liberally with her Evening in Paris scent. She always had a pile of Woman and Woman's Own magazines supplied by Maureen Qualter where we used to peruse the problem pages with great interest. Her long and happy marriage to Mick Madden ended with his death in 1990. Sarah, in her nineties, with her mind as sound as a bell, was still as much fun as ever up to her death in 2010.

The Qualter's house, Bina's kitchen and Hanley's Hall were also sources of entertainment. Bridgie and I once nearly died of fright coming home from Hanley's. Having been watching a spine chiller about the living dead we were witless with apprehension as we drew near the Graveyard and Friary ruins on the road back to Cregboy. We were aware of glittering eyes watching us from the hedgerows. Fox, owl, the undead, our imaginations provided the creepy music and every flicker or rustle in the air could only be vampire bats out hunting. The dark outline of the handball alley was identified by its aroma of stale urine, and a discarded sack could only be a crouching Bean Sí lying in wait.

Then we heard footsteps on the road behind us. We stopped, the footsteps stopped, we looked behind us, but it was too dark to see anything. We decided to make a run for it, which wasn't easy on an unlit, unmarked road with ditches on both sides and a fast flowing river to cross. We ran towards the welcoming light of Bina's, a beacon for weary travellers and lost souls. Whatever was following us was catching up. The moon came out from behind the clouds at this point, so we chanced a look back. We were being pursued by a big white faced Friesian cow.

Bridgie Duggan should have got more than three Hail Mary's as a penance at her next Confession.

I never knew Marteen as anything but a farmer. He was farming at twelve and had no great interest in anything else. He was my

monosyllabic cousin, a boy of few words, however when he did condescend to honour you with a conversation it was always worth hearing. He became a champion plough man, so Bridgie and I used to cycle to the local competitions to cheer him on. On one such occasion, and miles from home I got a puncture so was relieved to see him coming along with the horse and cart, and plenty of room beside the Pierce plough in the back. I'll take the bike or I'll take ye' he said,
'This horse has worked hard all day, and I'm not going to burden her with both' Love of horse, concern for cousin, no contest?

  Micheál's interest was hurling, hurling, or hurling but there was no way I was travelling miles to watch a hurling match. It was home matches in Hession's field only, and then only on a fine day. It was not so easy to avoid post mortems over the tea table.

Maureen and Winnie were polar opposites. Maureen would give you an opinion on anything, and often innocently told Aunt May things she didn't need to know. To start a sentence with 'Bina said' was to start a cross examination that would not have gone amiss at the Nuremburg Trials. Winnie was quiet and shy and having had a growth spurt that made her taller than Maureen she was often mistaken for being the older of the two. She hated conflict and would do anything to keep the peace. I have never come across anybody with a bad word to say about her. She died as she had lived, quietly at forty three, and much loved.

  Clinton cousins now came down for short holidays chauffeured by their father Christy and with their mother, Aunt Sheila in tow. Eamonn, as a young child had nearly died from diphtheria which had left him with a weak immune system, so as soon as his lungs came into contact with Claregalway air he would start to wheeze. I don't think he was ever there long enough for people to get to know his name. I got quite used to everybody calling him 'the sick wee ladeen'. His sister Carol was made of much tougher stuff and couldn't wait to see her mother on her way. Sheila dressed her like a little princess, frock with big bow, massive ribbons in her hair, neat little frilly white ankle socks and patent leather shoes, so soon as her Ma disappeared all went into her case, and only came out for Mass. She was soon as scruffy as the rest of us. I had reason to sympathise with Carol. Her Ma had been responsible for decking me out for my Confirmation in an aquamarine taffeta frock and an enormous black velvet Dutch bonnet.

I can still hear the taunts of the local kids as they recited an old skipping song for my benefit

'I'm a little Dutch girl dressed in blue,
Here are the actions I shall do;
Salute to the Officer'
Bow to the Queen,
Run around the corner for ice cream.

Chapter 41; The Copper Vase.

Every holiday I would make a point of visiting Uncle Séameen and Kerins back in Cloonbiggen. The little farm was neglected, and the thatch no longer had its shimmer of burnished gold, and long raided by rooks, it needed renewing. Kerins seemed disheartened and taciturn and Séameen's philosophy of 'Live for today, let tomorrow take care of its self' seemed to be in the ascendancy. I must have been about seventeen when I made a remark to Sarah that changed my whole perspective on the Cloonbiggen house. 'It's a wonder Kerins doesn't leave and get a job somewhere else' I said,
'Sure why would he' was Sarah's reply?
'Well Séameen can't be paying him very much' said I,
'*Why* would Séameen pay him' said Sarah, with surprise?
'For working the farm' said I,
'Why would ye pay family for working the farm, said she, when he has a share in it'?
It took about another ten questions of who, what, why, where, and when's to discover that Kerins was not a farm labourer but was Seanmháthair's child by a first marriage to Thomas Kearns. She had been widowed between the conception of Martin in 1900 and his birth in 1901, and had returned to live with her parents. When she married my grandfather Thomas Loftus in 1903, Martin stayed in Gortcloonmore with his grandmother Bridget Lenehan, widow of Tom Qualter, while his mother moved in to Tom Loftus's home further in the bog nearby. The mound of stones from that homestead still sits in isolation a few furlongs along from the Qualter ruins.
By the time Seanmháthair moved to nearby Cloonbiggen she had borne five Loftus children, Winifred, the oldest, dying in her early twenties in 1927 from tuberculosis meningitis. The Cloonbiggen move must have taken place sometime between Winifred's death in 1927 and Tom Loftus's death in 1933 because my mother was brought up in Gortcloonmore. 'Kerins' continued to live with his Grandmother until her death in 1923. How he became 'Kerins' and not 'Martin Kearns, my

eldest son, or Martin Kearns, my brother, or Martin Kearns, your Uncle'
is a mystery. Was there perhaps an element of the sins of the father?

When I talked about it to the Qualter's and the Duggan's they all
assumed I knew he was my Uncle, it was not a secret. When I talked to
him about it he just smiled and said

'Well, there's family, and there's family, and some are more fortunate
than others'.

I don't know what happened to his share in the farm, or whether he ever
acquired any land in his own right. He would have been too young to do
so under the Land Commission distribution. He spent his declining years
living with Pat Cullinan and his wife Una Monahan and their children in
Cahergowan. Suffice to say I remember him with great affection. His
claim to fame was that being born a child whose father had died before
his birth he was believed to be endowed with the ability to cure thrush.
Babies from far and wide were brought to him to have him breathe on
them.

His oft reiterated simple philosophy was 'take the day for what it's worth
and do the best ye can'. He did just that. In life he played the hand he
was given and didn't waste time wishing that he had been dealt
something else. He was a simple, kindly, honest, hardworking man which
should be enough of an epitaph.

Chapter 42; The Enigma

I have always had an interest in genealogy but it wasn't until I retired and became computer literate that I had the time to pursue it.

I chose to start with relatives, who had no direct descendents to remember them, 'The Invisible Man', 'Poor House Alice', and 'Little Orphan Annie' were top of the list. The Invisible Man was Martin Kearns father, Thomas. On Martin's birth certificate he was recorded as deceased, and according to family lore he was born in Craughwell, married in Claregalway and died from peritonitis in Gortcloonmore, all within Co. Galway. After a two year search of records and archives this man hadn't been born, hadn't married and hadn't died. The only thing stopping me from believing he was a figment of Seanmháthair's imagination was that she had been recorded as a widow on her marriage certificate to Tom Loftus.

My sole inheritance from Seanmháthair was a little copper vase. It was in the small package Sarah had given to me after the funeral. The inscription said 'Tiffany's, New York'. It is beautifully embossed and not the type of high class object you would expect to find down a bog road. I've always treasured it and often wondered how it got to Cloonbiggen. It took me more than sixty years to find the answer.

I sat looking at the vase one afternoon after another long and fruitless search of Irish Civil and Church marriages and as a last throw of the dice I entered the name Mary Bridget Qualter onto the International Genealogical Index, and there she was

Bridget Qualter married Thomas Kearns in Brooklyn, New York, on the 18th April 1897'. I must have read it ten times before I believed it. For some reason she registered her marriage as Bridget and not Mary Bridget her given name.

April 18th 1897	Brooklyn New York
Holy Rosary Church	Rev. P.J. Minogue
Groom – Thomas Kearns	Bride –* Bridget Qualter
Single 6☐ y	Mary Bridget Qualter 27y

61 Madison St.	138 E 124TH St.
Born Ireland	Born Ireland
Father; David Kearns	Father; Thomas Qualter
Mother; Margaret Flaherty	Mother; Bridget Lenehan
Witness; Cornelius Sullivan	Witness; Patrick O'Leary

I love a family mystery and found Seanmháthair's use of the name Bridget is not the only odd thing about the marriage certificate. Thomas's age is recorded as 60 but looks as if the person registering the ceremony initially wrote 65 and corrected the five to a zero. As for Seanmháthair I have been unable to authenticate with any certainty any trace of her entry into America but knowing that Martin had been born in Gortcloonmore she, and Thomas, must have returned to Ireland some time after the marriage in 1897. Eventually I found all three of them in Galway in 1900-1901.

By the time I got around to asking questions facts were hard to establish and difficult to substantiate but Sarah was so adamant that Thomas had died in Galway that I wrote to the archivist to see if his death had been missed off the national register. I was rewarded with a death certificate recording his death in Suckeen, a poor waterside area near Wood Quay in Galway City on the 22nd of November 1900, and two months before Martin's birth. The cause of his death was ascites as a result of liver failure, and was witnessed by Seanmháthair indicating he was not having Hospital care or ensconced in the Workhouse. By the time of the Census she and her two month old baby were recorded back in Gortcloonmore so the Suckeen address is unknown. However, looking at the inhabits of the 51 households listed familiar names like Feeney, Hession, Lenihan and Loftus are recorded, as is a boarder in No.31 David Kearns but with no known connection.

Liver failure has connotations with cirrhosis, and an implied lifestyle, however it has other causes, including malignancy, so it would be wrong to defame Thomas in death. His age at death is given as 66y and would be in keeping with a birth year circa 1835. Although Thomas' parents are recorded on his marriage certificate I have not been able to trace them or his place of birth in any records, nor have I been able to follow his footprints in America with any certainty, or find his last resting place. He may well have had a paupers funeral in Galway and be buried in Bohermore.

Seanmháthair on the other hand is buried with my grandfather Thomas Loftus and their daughter Winifred in the Friary graveyard. The grave was opened in 1985 to inter her son Martin Kearns to rest uneasily in their company. His father is no longer the 'Invisible Man' but is still very much a man of mystery. After an extensive five year search of records the only relevant Thomas Kearns I have found was a widower with three grown up children who lived in Brooklyn NY. However our Thomas is described as single on his marriage certificate to my grandmother, but if I accept that as untrue I also have to accept the information recorded about his parents may be a fabrication. There is also no evidence to suggest he was born in Craughwell despite Sarah's assertion but then she was not aware that Seanmháthair has ever travelled further than Galway City!

The unanswered questions to the mystery for me are;

Why did Seanmháthair end up in New York when she had a brother in Indiana and Lenihan cousins in Boston who would have sponsored her?

Did she initially emigrate to either of these places, if so, why did she move to New York?

Her address in East Harlem gives no clues to her occupation or living conditions. All it tells us is that it was in an area near Central Park that serviced the development of the elevated railroad which was extended to Harlem in 1880. With the construction of the "els," building of brownstones blocks of flats, taking the place of detached homes, occurred very rapidly, often without meeting planning regulations. Developers anticipated that the Lexington Avenue subway would ease transportation to lower Manhattan and would give them a lucrative return on their investment but fearing that new housing regulations would be enacted in 1901 they rushed to complete construction. However a delay in the building of the subway led to a fall in real estate prices scuppering their plans and attracting immigrant Eastern Europe Jews and Italians to Harlem in accelerating numbers. The rest is history.

So who sponsored her?

The only relevant ships document I have found in the quest to find her entry to America is for a 23 year old Mary Qualter (Quilter) travelling on the White Star 'Teutonic' from Queenstown to New York arriving 18th October 1893. This entry gives no other information apart from the fact that no agent or sponsor is noted so sponsorship is remains unknown

Why, four years later, would a good looking young woman of twenty seven marry a penniless man of sixty plus'?

The information on his marriage declaration at the Holy Rosary Parish Church in Brooklyn as to his age, previous marital status and the names of his parents is highly suspect which adds to this mystery.

Why return to live in a slum in Galway City, pregnant, and with a dying husband?

Was there an element of desperation in her return? Was it bound up with the unanswered question of our connections to the Drumgriffin Kelly's which I have yet to fathom? This may lie in the Kelly's family history and their Qualter connections. It could well be that Malachi, who owned pubs in Indianapolis, sponsored her as he did others. Over the years he made several trips back to Galway until the advent of Prohibition in America when he too returned to Drumgriffin with his wife and youngest children, and bought up 250 acres of the Ffrench Estate and the Central Tavern in Loughgeorge. He was the father of Roddy, my Godfather, who, until my mother's death, used to visit us in Dublin.

Until I can authenticate the documentation of her entry into America, or find evidence of her life there, these questions remain unanswered. The fact that she was not there for the 1880 or 1890 Censi doesn't help. Currently I know nothing more about that period in my Grandmother's life. I have no idea what she endured, only that she survived.

Does it matter that the questions remained unanswered? To me, yes. To the readers of this memoir, probably not; Thomas Kearns and Seanmháthair are long dead and gone, as is 'Kerins'.

Lionel Kearns, a Canadian poet with Irish roots puts my feelings in a nutshell in his poem 'Genealogy' from his collection *A Few Words Will Do*. I feel a kinship with him when he describes an ancestral search (quote);

Wispy scratches on microfilm attest
to a marriage here, a bris or baptism there,

the institutions whispering validity
to events once glistening with emotion,
saturated with colour, as large at least
as life, all shrunken now, withered
to a few notes in a base of data, faded
figures without clear features, dry
as pinned butterflies'.

To end on such a sad melancholy note would be fitting; however there *is* one unanswered question that I'm sure interests all of us and which remains a puzzle.

Why was my Ma 'called from the pulpit'?

Only the Canon and the Ma know for sure. Pre-supposing that they made it past St. Peter, I wonder, when they're looking down on Erin's green valley's from their mansions above, is she still trying to avoid him?

~ ~ ~ ~ ~

43; Requiescat in pace et amor

1881 Thomas Qualter.* Age 50 Gortcloonmore	
1900　Thomas Kearns.　Age 66 Galway	
1923　Bridget Qualter nee Lenihan.* Age 86 Gortcloonmore	
1932　Thomas Loftus.　Age 80 Cloonbiggen	
1942　Malachi Kelly.　Age 82 Drumgriffin	
1944　Mary Bridget Loftus nee Qualter.　Age 74 Cloonbiggen	
1946　Catherine (Kate) Lenihan nee Kelly.　Age 82 Claregalway	
1946　Canon (Pa) Moran.　Age 71 Lakeview	
1947　Julia Redmond nee Loftus.　Age 39 Dublin	
1947　Bridget (Delia) Moore nee Lenihan.　Age 43 Dublin	
1947　Tom Qualter.　Age 80 Indiana	

1948 Catherine Fletcher nee Qualter. Age 80 Gore NZ	
1949 John Redmond. Age 73 Dublin	
1949 Martin Qualter. Age 75 Gortcloonmore	
1950 John Qualter. Age 83 Lecarrowmore	
1951 Bridget (Bid) Greally. Age 76 Gortcloonmore	
1954 Bridget Qualter nee Noone. Age 73 Gortcloonmore	
1956 Mary (Molly) Cullinan. Cahergowan	
1963 Julia Keegan nee Qualter. Age 80 Indiana	
1966 Johnny Qualter. Age 40 Gortcloonmore	
1966 Michael Duggan. Age 65 Cregboy	
1970 Roddy Kelly. Age 69 Loughgeorge	
1971 Peter Greally. Age 87 Cloonbiggen	
1975 Christopher Clinton. Age 75 Dublin	

1975   Julia Redmond nee Byrne.   Age 93
Dublin

1975   Mary Casserly.   Age 66
Cregboy

1979   Sabina (Bina) Lenihan.   Age 70
Claregalway

1981 Sabina (Bin-e) Greally. Age 87
Cloonbiggen

1983   Peter Redmond.   Age 74
Dublin

1983   Tommy Duggan.   Age 45
Cregboy

1985   Winnie Reddington nee Duggan.   Age 43
Cregboy

1885   Martin Kearns.   Age 84
Cahergowan

1985   Mattie Carr.   Age 55
Cregboy

1987   Pat Cullinan.   Age 63
Cahergowan

1988   Malachy 'Lackie' Qualter. Age 71
Gortcloonmore

1991   James 'Séameen' Loftus.   Age 85

Cloonbiggen	
1995 May Duggan nee Loftus. Age 84 Cregboy	
1999 Tom Qualter. Age 84 Gortcloonmore	
2001 Winnie Qualter. Age 80 Gortcloonmore	
2003 Mary Duggan nee Kelly. Age 83 Waterdale	
2004 Willie Forde. Age 88 Gortcloonmore	
2008 Maureen Qualter. Age 87 Gortcloonmore	
2009 Seán Redmond. Age 66 Malaysia	Dublin / Australia /
2010 Sarah Madden. Age 94 Galway	
2011 Bridgie Glynn nee Duggan. Age 77 Belclare	Guarrane
2011 Eileen Cullinan. Age 80 Cahergowan	Carrowkeel
Buried in Creggs	

TENANTS IN THE TOWNLAND OF GORTCLOONMORE 1847-64 (Griffith Valuation)*
Matthias Duggan ~
William Duggan ~
John Feeney ~
Martin Feeney ~
Timothy Feeney ~
William Feeney ~
Jeremiah Grealy ~
John Grealy ~
William Grealy ~
Mary Noon ~
Thomas Qualter ~ Bridget Lenehan

*Landlord: James S Lambert; Placenames: An Loch bheag.
Gortcloonmore adjoins the Waterdale River on the north side and
Montiagh North at the other end. Gortcloonmore is mainly low
lying but has a mixture of land ranging from good grazing pastures
to bog. Turf is cut there and in the past it supplied many
households in the parish.

Gortcloonmore Census 1901-1911

Families in Townland

1901 Grealy William 68 Male Head of Family

Grealy Mary 50 Female Wife

Grealy Patrick 26 Male Son

Grealy Margaret 24 Female Daughter

Grealy Bridget 22 Female Daughter

Grealy Norah 21 Female Daughter

Grealy Ellen 19 Female Daughter

Grealy Mary 17 Female Daughter

Grealy John 15 Male Son

Grealy Sarah 12 Female Daughter

1911 Greally William 47 Male Head of Family

Greally Bridget 40 Female Wife

Greally Darby 11 Male Son

Greally Sabina 9 Female Daughter

Greally Mary 8 Female Daughter

Greally Bridget 6 Female Daughter

Greally Maria 4 Female Daughter

Greally Patrick 1 Male Son

Duggan Martin 42 Male Brother in Law

1901 Grealy Darby 80 Male Head of Family

Grealy William 35 Male Son

Grealy Bridget 32 Female Daughter in law

Grealy Sarah 30 Female Daughter

Grealy Michal 24 Male Son

Browne George 9 Male Nephew

Grealy Darby Male Grand Son

1911 Greally Mary 65 Female Head of Family

Greally Patrick 38 Male Son

Greally Bridget 30 Female Daughter

Greally Ellen 27 Female Daughter

Greally Sarah 23 Female Daughter

1901 Qualter Bridget 65 Female Head of Family

Qualter Martin 25 Male Son

Qualter William 23 Male Son

Qualter Julia 19 Female Daughter

Kerins nee Qualter Mary 28 Female Daughter

Kerins (Kearns) Martin Male Grand Son

1901 Loftus Thomas 47 Male Head of Family

1911 Loftus Thomas 63 Male Head of Family

Loftus Mary 42 Female Wife nee Qualter - Kerins

Loftus James 5 Male Son

Loftus Winifred 7 Female Daughter

Loftus Julia 4 Female Daughter

Loftus Margaret Female Daughter

1901 Duggan Martin 73 Male Head of Family

Duggan Julia 73 Female Wife

Duggan James 50 Male Son

Duggan Bridget 32 Female Daughter in Law

Duggan Julia 3 Female Grand Daughter

Duggan Martin 1 Male Grand Son

1911 Duggan Martin 80 Male Head of Family

Duggan Julia 80 Female Wife

Duggan James 52 Male Son

Duggan Bridget 44 Female Daughter in Law

Duggan Julia 13 Female Grand Daughter

Duggan Martin 12 Male Grand Son

1901 Duggan Henry 74 Male Head of Family

Duggan Bridget 60 Female Wife

Duggan Tady 36 Male Son

Duggan Mary 32 Female Daughter in Law

Duggan Kate 19 Female Daughter Roman Catholic

1911 Duggan Henry 84 Male Head of Family

Duggan Bridget 72 Female Wife

Duggan Thady 47 Male Son in Law

Duggan Kate 29 Female Daughter

Duggan Mary 44 Female Daughter

Duggan Harry 7 Male Grand Son

Duggan Michael 4 Male Grand Son

Duggan Patrick 1 Male Grand Son

1901 Feeney Margaret 70 Female Head of Family

Feeney Peter 57 Male Son

Feeney Bridget 32 Female Daughter in Law

Feeney Martin 28 Male Son

Feeney Timothy 8 Male Grand Son

Feeney Sarah 7 Female Grand Daughter

Feeney Michael 5 Male Grand Son

Feeney Patrick 3 Male Grand Son

1901 Feeney John 30 Male Head of Family

Feeney Bridget 34 Female Sister

1901 Flaherty Michael 80 Male Head of Family

Flaherty Sarah 60 Female Wife

Flaherty Martin 37 Male Son

Flaherty Sarah 30 Female Daughter in Law

Flaherty Norah 20 Female Daughter

Flaherty Mary Kate Female Grand Daughter

1901 Glennane Mathias 64 Male Head of Family

Glennane Bridget 63 Female Wife

Glennane Sabina 33 Female Daughter

Glennane William 32 Male Son

Glennane Kate 22 Female Daughter

Glennane Andrew 20 Male Son

OTHER MEMOIRS

I DREAMT I DWELT IN MARBLE HALLS (Memoir)

The rent of 3s.6p a week in the Dublin Artisans' Dwelling Company flats was relatively high in the early 1920's when the author's grandparents moved in. Built to house artisans the tenancies were beyond the means of labourer's who earned about a £1 a week.

On the death of her mother in 1947 she moved from nearby Upper Rutland St. to live in the Dwellings with her grandparents and remembers it as a matriarchal enclave where the women castigated and cursed each other's children and minded them when necessary. They criticized one another, supported one another through the 'nagers', delivered babies when a 'Bona Fide' midwife wasn't available or couldn't be afforded, borrowed and lent finery, often taken out of the Pawn for the occasion, and laid out and waked the dead. The Memoir is rich in humour and historical lore for those who remember Summerhill, the Dwellings, the nearby Streets, the Tin Church, and the choice of schools like the Red Brick Slaughter House, the Sado Brothers or the love 'em or hate 'em Nuns in North William Street. It will lead you down a path of nostalgia you cannot fail to enjoy. For others it's a series of glimpses of North Dublin communal life that for once does not include vermin, abuse, neglect or a granny who was a dealer. It also encompasses vignettes of family members bringing them to life to be remembered fondly with wry recognition of their faults and foibles. We are introduced to characters like Annie Lawlor, Nick Colgan and the Grant and Breslin families and will meet some of them again in 'Thrown on Life's Surge'.

THROWN ON LIFE'S SURGE (Memoir)

This memoir is part of an Irish trilogy based on the experience and recollections of the author, a Dublin girl from Summerhill, a decaying north inner city area a short walk from the City Centre. Her first volume provides a glimpse of a Dublin childhood and family life in the Artisans Dwellings, Upper Buckingham Street in 1940's -1950's Dublin, and the second, in complete contrast, an account of running wild in the boglands of Galway during the long summer holidays. This volume covers the period of a nurse training course at St. Anne's Skin and Cancer Hospital. There, age 17y, she learned to deal with the terminally ill on a daily basis in a setting that provided dignity, comfort, camaraderie and, more surprisingly, fun.

The Nuns, her fellow probationers and the patients are all portrayed as people well remembered. The Nuns range from the 'She Devil' to the saintly and the probationers as culchie's to the core, united in their urge to escape bondage on the family farm. Stories of the patients are poignant, in particular those of Mikeen and Maggo. In contrast the humour of the deaths of Mrs. Von and the Widow Maker, and the hilarity of a Day at the Races is life affirming and funny.

PEA SOUP AND JELLIED EELS (Memoir)

The scene changes from the Dublin of the previous trilogy as the author arrives in Poplar in 1957 to train as a nurse in St. Andrews Hospital in Bromley-by-Bow. In doing so she ignored the dire warnings of the Matron of a Dublin Hospital where she was undertaking a pre-training course that the East End slums were a hotbed of depravity. However never one to kow-tow to authority her meeting with Grace Laing on a recruitment drive decided her fate. At a time when a home grown supply of trainees were in short supply English hospital Matrons went to Ireland on recruitment drives. It was in Dublin's grand hotel lounges the Matrons scrutinised and interrogated prospective recruits while consuming coffee and biscuits. In Bernadette's case this ended up with a choice of hospitals in Birmingham, Liverpool, London and Manchester. It was Grace Laing; the Matron of St. Andrews Hospital in London, whose genuine interest in the prospective trainee's individual backgrounds and reasons for emigrating that decided her choice. London's East End it was.

This memoir of her SRN training is humourous, knowledgeable and a snapshot in time of a much loved District Hospital, inspiring Matron, dedicated staff and appreciative patients. However this is not a rose tinted retrospective. There are no ministering angels here. Long hours and hard work put paid to that. Back street abortions, terrible injuries on the docks, chronic bronchitis, tuberculosis and life threatening childhood diseases were the reality of nursing life in an era of primitive diagnostic equipment and pharmacology in its infancy. Her description of the Juju Men is priceless as is her encounter with 'the Randy Dandy'. Other sadder tales overshadowed by the spectre of death are remembered with empathy.

For those of you looking for a stereotypical view of East End slums, misery and crime ridden neighbourhoods this is not the book for you. This East End paints a picture of a vibrant, resilient hard working people, as were the majority of East Enders. Yes, some lived in dire poverty but a spirit of camaraderie predominated, and survived being re-housed in far flung suburbs returning weekly to buy pie and mash and shop 'up the Roman'.

The author spent 25 years in Community Nursing in Tower Hamlets retiring in 2004. She still lives in Bethnal Green and remains a true East Ender.

A PROMISE OF TOMORROWS (Memoir)

As the author moves on with her dreams of a career in nursing on hold the scene shifts from London's East End across the river to the leafy suburbs of south-east London then onwards and upwards to the Mecca of the medical profession in the golden triangle that was Harley St, Wimpole St and Devonshire Place.

Working as a nanny cum housekeeper for two ambitious doctors and living en famille she takes on the responsibility of their six anarchic, unruly, bickering, lovable children.

She charts their family life through the ups and downs of thirteen eventful years with humour and perception as the children protest her authority and find ingenious ways of circumventing her boundaries. Disappearing, as they were wont to do at the first sign of battle, one is left to wonder wryly why their parents had six children in the first place, since their parenting seemed peripheral to their busy professional lives. Their upward mobility was not without its tribulations or effects on family life.

Told with humour and perspicuity this is a book all grown up naughty children will enjoy. Chapters with headings like 'What part of NO don't you understand' or 'I don't care who started it' are sure to bring back memories for many, as will sibling rivalry and surviving accidents, poisonings and explosions.